# Muncie 4-Speed Transmissions

## How to Rebuild and Modify

**Paul Cangialosi**

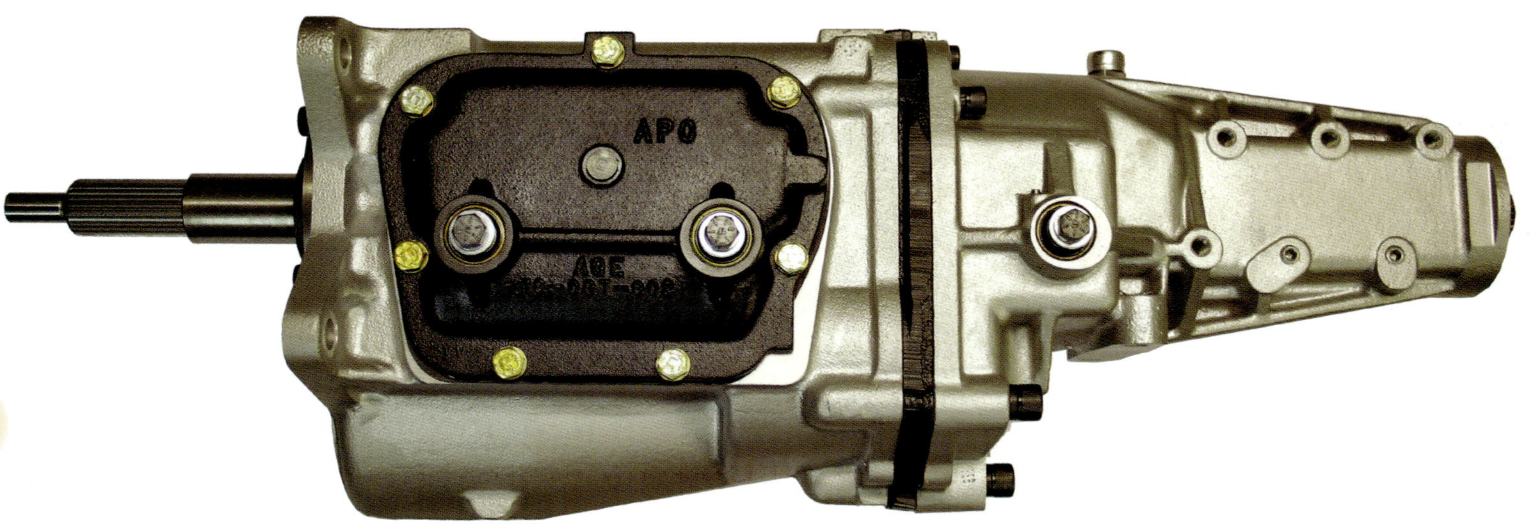

***CarTech*®**

# CarTech®

CarTech®, Inc.
6118 Main St.
North Branch, MN 55056
Phone: 651-277-1200 or 800-551-4754
Fax: 651-277-1203
www.cartechbooks.com



Edit by Paul Johnson
Layout by Chris Fayers

ISBN 978-1-61325-106-5
Item No. SA278

Library of Congress Cataloging-in-Publication Data

Cangialosi, Paul.
  Muncie 4-speed transmissions / by Paul Cangialosi.
     pages cm
  Includes bibliographical references and index.
  ISBN 978-1-61325-106-5 (alk. paper)
1.  General Motors automobiles--Transmission devices. 2.  General Motors automobiles--Transmission devices--Maintenance and repair.  I. Title. II. Title: Muncie four-speed transmissions.

TL262.C364 2014
629.2›44--dc23
2014009741

Written, edited, and designed in the U.S.A.
Printed in China
10 9 8 7

---



**Front Cover:**
*State-of-the-art replacement Muncie case components and gears set a new standard for rebuilding an old, worn-out Muncie 4-speed.*

**Title Page:**
*This is a completed SPEC-25. The special Teflon coating reduces internal friction and heat: The exterior becomes a non-stick surface and gasket surfaces clean up very quickly. Plans are in the works for new-style NASCAR synchro assemblies and more ratios, so a SPEC-35 will most definitely be in the future!*

**Back Cover Photos:**

**Top**
*Usually the gear and 3-4 synchro hub dislodge if you hold third gear and gently tap on the front of the mainshaft. Later units have hardened hubs with extremely tight press fits, and you must use a press to remove them. If the gear and hub do not come off, do not use a hammer to try to remove them. The tip of the mainshaft is easily damaged. Use a press and bearing clamp on third gear for removal.*

**Middle:**
*Lift the countergear out of the case. If the case was damaged from a gear explosion, the thrust washers are often jammed from debris. If that has happened, stand the case on its front face, so that the loose gear doesn't cock or move off center, and rotate it as you remove it.*

**Bottom Left:**
*The bronze synchro ring has a 6-degree internal taper that matches the taper on the gear's synchro cone. As it is forced up against the cone, it eventually causes the output shaft to run at the same speed as the gear. It's essentially a cone clutch.*

**Bottom Right:**
*I never press directly on gear surfaces. The lower gear has an old bearing race against it. This grabs closer to the inside diameter of the gear to prevent press-surface contact with the gear teeth.*

DISTRIBUTION BY:
*Europe*
PGUK
63 Hatton Garden
London EC1N 8LE, England
Phone: 020 7061 1980 • Fax: 020 7242 3725
www.pguk.co.uk
*Australia*
Renniks Publications Ltd.
3/37-39 Green Street
Banksmeadow, NSW 2109, Australia
Phone: 2 9695 7055 • Fax: 2 9695 7355
www.renniks.com
*Canada*
Login Canada
300 Saulteaux Crescent
Winnipeg, MB, R3J 3T2 Canada
Phone: 800 665 1148 • Fax: 800 665 0103
www.lb.ca

# CONTENTS

# ACKNOWLEDGMENTS

When CarTech offered me a contract to write a book on Muncies I thought to myself that it is something I do every day, and it will be an easy task. *Wrong*! It took longer than anticipated. I had many setbacks, both on a personal and a business level. I'd like to thank my editor Paul Johnson and CarTech for their support and belief in me.

Brian Higgins of the SK Tranny Shop allowed me to crawl around his parts photographing some archeological finds. His place was mind blowing as usual. Thank you, Brian, for allowing me to interrupt your busy schedule.

Larry Fischer, a true legend and a long-time friend, also took some time to drag out parts and talk about his experiences.

Ed Hartnett was instrumental in sending me pictures of his rare 3864848 cases. I thank him for putting up with my nagging to get the perfect shot.

George Sollish of Auto Gear is the man responsible for bringing back the Muncie. I'd like to personally thank him and his hard-working staff: Robin, Matt, Nathan, Billy, Howie, Joe, and the cats. Without them there would be no future for this transmission and I'd still be playing drums in some crappy punk-rock band.

The late James Fodrea, who was credited for the design of the Muncie, gave many others and me a career in manual transmissions. I give sincere thanks to his daughter, Joan Fodrea Cooper, for taking the time to talk about her father and his days at General Motors.

My biggest realization in writing this book came from seeing how unorganized my shop really is compared with everyone else's. My webmaster, Janet, aka '"Gear Rhonda," still makes it a point to insult me every day in front of hundreds of web clientele. She inspires me to continue to push myself and set unrealistic goals.

Cristina, one day all this will be yours!

# INTRODUCTION

You have purchased this book because you want to learn about the Muncie 4-speed. I was chosen to write this book because I have been involved with rebuilding, manufacturing replacement parts, and selling completely new replacement 4-speed Muncies for 34 years.

Writing this book has been an interesting journey and I have met a lot of people along the way. One thing that I must point out before I start going into technical details is that if not for all the people I met buying, selling, rebuilding, and manufacturing parts for these transmissions, I probably would not have been in this line of work. Many people have transitioned their love for Muncies into viable businesses, or in some cases, great supplementary income. The Muncie was used in GM vehicles from 1963 to early 1975. The number of these transmissions is staggering. Hundreds of thousands of Muncie 4-speeds were produced and no other 4-speed in the world comes close to those numbers.

In 1979 I was one of *those* hobbyists. I purchased loads of Muncie cores at local car shows and started rebuilding them with parts scavenged from other transmissions. I purchased inventory from auto parts stores that were liquidating new gears. In those days, junkyards used to rebuild transmissions with cores they had on hand. It was the same thing I was doing, except they had a lot more space and inventory. When these businesses got out of rebuilding, I ended up purchasing their inventory and new parts. I had acquired a few hundred Muncie transmissions and loads of parts. I also had Ford and Mopar transmissions but, honestly, the demand was just not there at that time. Because these transmissions were relatively untouched I got to see the pattern of how they were put together. For example, I learned how certain case components were mated to other parts and what type of bolt logos were used during certain years.

A few Corvette collectors contacted me about authenticating their transmissions. I recall they were 1963 and 1966 Z06 "Big Tank" cars. I started rebuilding transmissions for a number of Corvette collectors and shops during that period. One owner suggested that I go to the Corvettes at Carlisle show and sell my rebuild kits to the public. At the time I had a full-time job as a mechanical engineer and never really sold at car shows; I was always buying. I did notice that nobody was selling anything new. Typically, most used parts were laid out on a blanket, unclean, and with some price sticker on them. There was endless used stuff around but nothing available new for sale to repair or to rebuild these transmissions.

In 1981, I took my friend's advice. I started by selling gasket and seal kits as well as complete rebuild kits for Muncies at 14 car shows that year. I quit my job. The car-show routine went on for 12 years. I had also added a few complete rebuilt transmissions to make up a nice, attractive, eye-catching display. Much to my surprise, I sold out often. Working 14 shows a year for 12 years, you meet a lot of people and see loads of parts. You get invited to things, including the 10th anniversary of GM's Bowling Green Plant or just having breakfast one day with Zora Arkus-Duntov and his wife Elfi. All this from a bunch of greasy parts!

The concept of this book is to give you some history about the Muncie and how the transmission evolved from 1963 to 1974. Identifying the type of Muncie you have is important because most correct automotive restorations demand the correct transmission. This is something that is regularly overlooked. Frequently, cars advertised as "matching numbers cars" don't have the correct transmission. Both the history and identification sections of this book aid you in learning about this process. You will also learn how to completely rebuild a Muncie, inspect for worn parts, and make necessary repairs.

A complete parts breakdown with three-dimensional diagrams is at the end of Chapter 8. The actual GM patent for the Muncie is in the Appendix.

Muncies have been mentioned in many automotive restoration books. The cut-and-paste culture of the Internet has created overnight "experts" out of novices who copy information (often incorrect) onto home-brewed websites selling transmissions and parts. You can also find many self-proclaimed experts who offset free erroneous advice on blogs and automotive Internet forums every day.

For some reason, people expect that free videos and free information on the Internet will be high quality. This book is not free. It took time and money to research, obtain photos, and write. Visit my support page at MuncieBook.com. I welcome any feedback (positive or negative) you might have, and will answer any of your questions. I sincerely thank you, the reader, for recognizing the value of this book.

# WHAT IS A WORKBENCH® BOOK?

This Workbench® Series book is the only book of its kind on the market. No other book offers the same combination of detailed hands-on information and revealing color photographs to illustrate transmission rebuilding. Rest assured, you have purchased an indispensable companion that will expertly guide you, one step at a time, through each important stage of the rebuilding process. This book is packed with real world techniques and practical tips for expertly performing rebuild procedures, not vague instructions or unnecessary processes. At-home mechanics or enthusiast builders strive for professional results, and the instruction in our Workbench® Series books help you realize pro-caliber results. Hundreds of photos guide you through the entire process from start to finish, with informative captions containing comprehensive instructions for every step of the process.

The step-by-step photo procedures also contain many additional photos that show how to install high-performance components, modify stock components for special applications, or even call attention to assembly steps that are critical to proper operation or safety. These are labeled with unique icons. These symbols represent an idea, and photos marked with the icons contain important, specialized information.

Here are some of the icons found in Workbench® books:

***Important!—***
Calls special attention to a step or procedure, so that the procedure is correctly performed. This prevents damage to a vehicle, system, or component.

***Save Money—***
Illustrates a method or alternate method of performing a rebuild step that will save money but still give acceptable results.

***Torque Fasteners—***
Illustrates a fastener that must be properly tightened with a torque wrench at this point in the rebuild. The torque specs are usually provided in the step.

***Special Tool—***
Illustrates the use of a special tool that may be required or can make the job easier (caption with photo explains further).

***Performance Tip—***
Indicates a procedure or modification that can improve performance. Step most often applies to high-performance or racing engines.

***Critical Inspection—***
Indicates that a component must be inspected to ensure proper operation of the engine.

***Precision Measurement—***
Illustrates a precision measurement or adjustment that is required at this point in the rebuild.

***Professional Mechanic Tip—***
Illustrates a step in the rebuild that non-professionals may not know. It may illustrate a shortcut, or a trick to improve reliability, prevent component damage, etc.

***Documentation Required—***
Illustrates a point in the rebuild where the reader should write down a particular measurement, size, part number, etc. for later reference or photograph a part, area or system of the vehicle for future reference.

***Tech Tip—***
Tech Tips provide brief coverage of important subject matter that doesn't naturally fall into the text or step-by-step procedures of a chapter. Tech Tips contain valuable hints, important info, or outstanding products that professionals have discovered after years of work. These will add to your understanding of the process, and help you get the most power, economy, and reliability from your engine.

# HISTORY AND EVOLUTION

*This is a classic Muncie bolt pattern and case. It's a standard M20 model.*

To understand the evolution of the Muncie 4-speed you have to look at a series of engineering platforms that led to the final design of this transmission. The Muncie design has roots going back to 1935. I took the time to research the patent number that is cast into most Muncie main cases. It is U.S. Patent Number 3,088,336 (see Appendix). You will see that James W. Fodrea designed the patent; no other engineers are listed. If you look closely, you'll see that the patent drawings look nothing like the Muncie 4-speed but rather like the BorgWarner T10! Therefore, the Muncie patent is basically a design for the layout of a 4-speed transmission. This "layout" is a 4-speed trans-

mission with four forward gear ratios in the main case, a midplate bearing support, and a reverse gearset in the extension housing.

BorgWarner was a company founded in 1928 from the merger of Borg and Beck (founded in 1904) and Warner Gear (founded in 1901). They designed a 3-speed transmission, the T85, which was originally used in the 1935 Chrysler Airflow. It was used right up to 1971 in the Ford Pickup F100 with an overdrive. The T10 shares the same case design, gear centers, and 3-4 synchronizer as the T85. The cases have a distinctive similar size, shape, and cover-bolt pattern.

If you look at Fodrea's 4-speed patent drawings you can clearly see it was based on the T85 platform. His brilliant and well-thought-out idea was to make it into a 4-speed. It's important to understand that in 1956 General Motors didn't have the money for the Corvette program. Zora Arkus-Duntov wanted to use the design of General Motors' employee James Fodrea. BorgWarner was probably the foremost manual transmission manufacturer at the time, and basically wrote the book on manual transmission design. (They are credited with hundreds of

*James Fodrea and Alice Henman are on the way to visit the Muncie plant in 1957. Fodrea was the GM engineer whose name is listed on the design patent for the Muncie. Although he is seen with a 1957 Corvette, which came with a T10 4-speed, the design of the T10 and Muncie share the same features.*

manual transmission patents.) It is therefore no surprise that a decision was made for BorgWarner to manufacture this 4-speed transmission based on the GM concept drawings and Fodrea's patent. It was a very logical decision: Tooling costs would be minimal because hobs, castings, and certain components could be used from the T85 platform. This would be the fastest and most cost-effective way to put a 4-speed into a Corvette with very little risk. Many Corvette

*This is how the Muncie countergear's design evolved. The center gear is from a BorgWarner T85 3-speed. The lower gear is the latest version of the early T10 and the upper is the Muncie M22. Note how the Muncie gear is physically longer than the T10. The reason for these design changes was simply to meet the demand for increased torque capacity.*

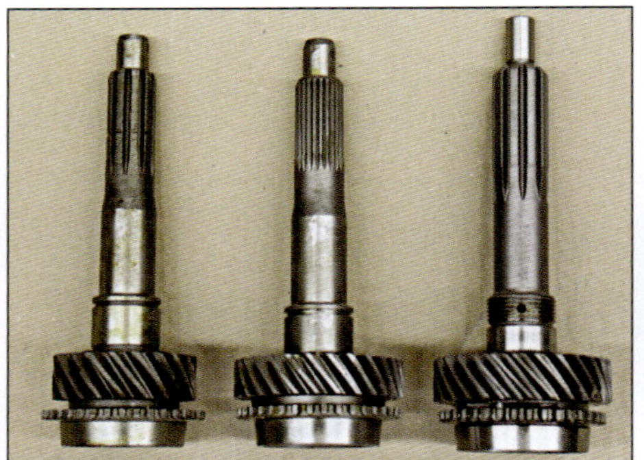

*The maindrive gear on the left is from a T85 3-speed. The center gear is from an early T10 and on the right is an M21 Muncie gear. All of these gears have the same number of clutch teeth: 36. Notice that the Muncie synchro cone is larger in diameter for improved stopping power.*

*This is the current Super T10 design. Its concept and design are identical to the Muncie's. Both were derived from the same U.S. patent.*

*This is the current Muncie M22. Your can see that the layout of the geartrain is identical to the ST10's. All gears and synchronizers are in the same position. Notice how the angle of the M22 gears is much straighter than on the ST10. The noise level increased because of this angle, giving the M22 the nickname "RockCrusher."*

restoration books share the common misconception that the 4-speed T10 and Muncie are two separate entities. They are not; the Muncie evolved from the T10.

## Happy Accidents Create the Muncie

The 4-speed design of the T10 and Muncie is a very "forward" design. Whether it was a series of lucky choices, or happy accidents, the 1957 design allowed for improvements. Other muscle car transmissions of that era, such as the Ford Toploader and Mopar A833, left no room for improvements because of the layout and initial design of their

geartrains. The Super T10 was a later-version design of the T10.

BorgWarner sold the T10 to Doug Nash in the early 1980s, which then sold it to Richmond Gear. In 2012, Motive Gear acquired Richmond Gear and they are still manufacturing the Super T10 today. Several NASCAR transmissions, such as the G-Force T101, are also T10-based. The Muncie saw many improvements during its 10-year production run with General Motors. Auto Gear Equipment (AGE) currently produces Muncie replacement parts as well as new replacement transmissions. Auto Gear sells them directly and also through approved distributors. Auto Gear's "Syracuse 4-speed" is a Muncie on steroids.

General Motors received royalties for every T10 sold from BorgWarner, so you have to wonder why they would bother making their own 4-speed at the Muncie plant. It appears that BorgWarner had an exclusivity contract with General Motors until 1960. This was the first year that the T10 was used in

the Ford Galaxie and Fairlane. Soon after, Chrysler and American Motors began using the T10. With the power levels increasing in GM muscle cars the power capacity of the T10 also needed to increase.

I believe the reasons for bringing the T10 to the Muncie plant were threefold. First was to revamp the T10 to handle more power. Second was the direct benefit of the increased sales volume of the 4-speed GM muscle car market. The third reason was increased T10 royalty benefits.

## Muncie Design Changes

Good engineering should allow for improvement to the design. When designing transmissions you have to remember that as vehicles change dynamically (increased horsepower, weight, or gas mileage requirements) the transmission also has to change. Because the Muncie was well engineered, there was room for improvement to the base design. Modern automation gives companies the ability to store incredible amounts of data; it's much easier to track changes. Today's VINs (vehicle identification numbers) are even bar coded. A service technician can use a scanner to find a VIN, and any known service issues are easily found.

From the 1960s until the late 1980s General Motors issued Technical Service Bulletins by mail or fax to alert dealerships of potential service issues. I'm not a fan of these but I do understand their importance. I do not like them because, for the most part, they are admitting defects to a design. They fix it if there is a complaint but do not order a recall. Recalls are bad publicity, so it's easier to fix the problem silently rather than risk sales. The problem is that some cars just aren't driven very often. The service issues crop up after the warranty period has expired and the owner is left to pay for a repair on something that was defective in the first place.

In the early 1980s I did a great deal of repair work for GM dealers nationwide for the Corvette 4+3 overdrive. It had three major service issues affecting 1984 and 1985 models. I had the bulletins, but most

*The first front-bearing retainer on the 1963 Muncie was made of aluminum; its casting number was 3790278. These proved to be very weak and were replaced by a cast-iron retainer (604932). Both of these retainers are now extremely rare.*

of these service issues happened after the warranty period ended.

I bring this up so you can better understand how service updates and design changes are handled. You also need to remember that all record keeping was done manually and sometimes the changes were left undocumented. It is often very difficult to decipher what part numbers actually match the part you may need because the GM parts books have discrepancies.

### 1963

The first Muncie has several unique features that were dropped by 1964. It had a small 6207-style front bearing and an aluminum front bearing retainer. This retainer was upgraded to cast iron by the end of the 1963 run. The 3831704 cast main case is unique because the front bore is smaller than it is on later Muncies. The first-speed gear rode directly on the mainshaft. A snap ring retained the first and second synchronizer assembly on the mainshaft. The first-speed gear had a smaller bore diameter as well as a recess in the bore to clear the synchronizer retaining snap ring. It had a thrust washer behind first gear that floated on the rear bearing inner race.

The countershaft diameter of 7/8 inch and front bearing were both

carried over from the T10 4-speed design. The shifter shafts had 5/16-18 threaded studs.

The GM service manuals are interesting. For some reason, the unique 1963-only items were still used in exploded-view illustrations, which confused many rebuilders into the early 1970s.

*This is not a Muncie 4-speed retainer. It is from a Saginaw 3-speed, casting number 591620. It can be used as an adapter-bearing retainer. It was an old trick to enable small-retainer transmissions to correctly pilot to large-retainer-bore bellhousings. If you attach a small-retainer transmission to a large-bore bellhousing the transmission is not piloted correctly. Typically, the front bearings shatter and input shafts break teeth, usually at the end if this mistake is made. This adapter retainer can be used to attach a 1963 Muncie to a later bellhousing. You can also turn down the outside diameter on a lathe to replace the rare 3790278 or 604932 retainers.*

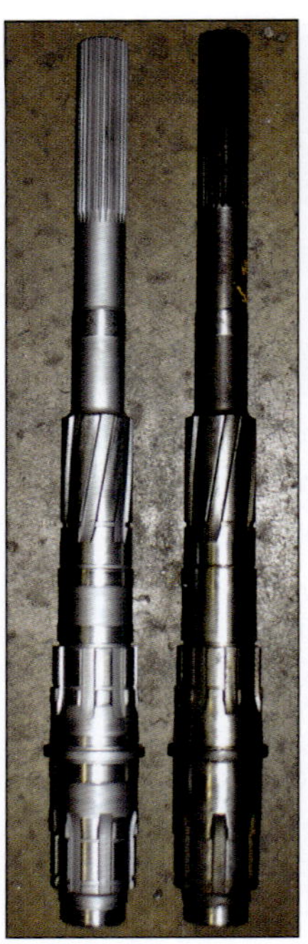

*Two 1963 Muncie mainshafts are shown here. An original 1963 shaft is shown at right while a rare BorgWarner replacement shaft is at left; it has an added oil cavity on the first-gear section. Notice that these shafts only have enough room for the speedometer drivegear to press onto them in one place. This means that they can only be used with extension housings that have a driver-side speedometer gear.*

The Muncie was designed to shift better than the T10; it used larger-diameter synchro cones. Both the M20 wide-ratio and M21 close-ratio transmissions were offered. These were the only ratios ever offered from General Motors for the Muncie 4-speed:

- M20 first, 2.56:1; second, 1.91:1; third, 1.48:1; fourth, 1.0:1; and reverse, 2.64:1

*These are three first-speed Muncie gears. The far left gear is a 1963 type that has the recess for the 1-2 synchronizer snap ring and a smaller bore. The middle gear is the later-style original-equipment late-1964 to 1974 gear. On the right is an aftermarket gear made in China.*

- M21 first, 2.20:1; second, 1.64:1; third, 1.28:1; fourth, 1.0:1; and reverse, 2.27:1

### 1964–1965

Two major improvements were issued. The first was the introduction of a larger-diameter front bearing that meant a new case casting and larger-diameter front bearing retainer were necessary. The second was that the first-speed gear now rode on a bushing that was press-fit onto the mainshaft. It stopped against the first and second synchronizer assembly, thereby eliminating the need for the assembly to have a retaining snap ring. Because the bushing was subsequently retained by the rear bearing, the synchronizer could not go anywhere. The first-gear thrust washer was eliminated and the gear was designed to have a thrust surface that ran against the rear bearing's inner race.

The first-gear design change was done for several reasons. The first was added strength. Whenever you have a snap-ring groove between a flow of power you have a potential stress riser on the shaft. Because the slider engages first gear across the snap-ring groove, a huge stress riser develops that leads to broken mainshafts. First gear also had a tendency to seize to the mainshaft. Cutting grooves and valleys for oil in the shaft only weakened the shaft more. A bushing was used with a "v" notch to promote better oil flow under the gear.

By the end of 1965 the rear extension housing saw some modifications to the casting. Webbing was added to the top and bottom. Small changes in countergear needle bearing spacer tubes surfaced. Some tubes were seamless with four needle spacers while others had a seam

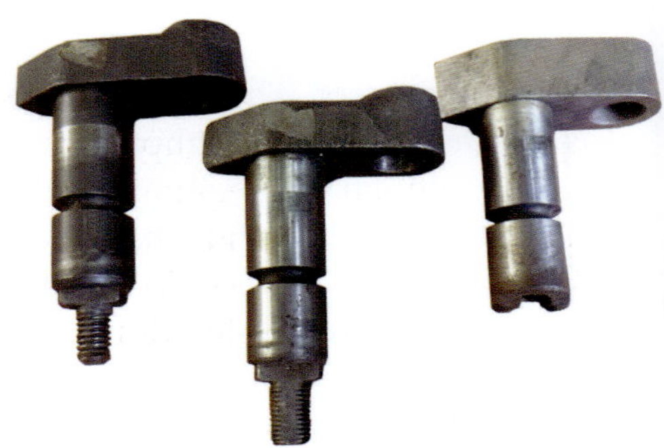

*Muncie shifter shafts have evolved in three basic stages. From the left, the small 5/16-18 threaded stud, which snapped easily. The newer 3/8-24 stud still had to fit the rectangular keyway of the linkage arm, and so it had flats milled on each side, but they still broke. The last revision was a bolt-on shaft using a standard 3/8-16 threaded hex head bolt.*

with six spacers. There seems to be no specific time when this change took place. By 1965 the shifter-shaft designs changed because they had been snapping. The new thread size of the stud was increased to 3/8-24.

*These spacer tubes go inside the countergear. The upper tube has no seam but the lower one does. Because the needle bearings ride against the seam, extra spacer rings are needed to cover the seam. Typically, the seamless spacer had four needle-spacer rings. The seamed spacer tube used six. Most of the later GM overhaul shop manuals show four spacers in the exploded-view diagrams when, in fact, the transmissions used six.*

In 1964 and 1965, Muncies in some of the full-size Chevrolet Impalas and Pontiac Catalinas were equipped with longer mainshafts and extension housings to keep driveshafts shorter and reduce harmonic vibration.

### M22 RockCrusher

In 1963 the Corvette Grand Sport racing program was instituted. The early Grand Sports used a special heavy-duty version of the M21 close-ratio transmission. These special units evolved into what is called the M22 today. According to research by Alan Colvin (author of the *Chevrolet by the Numbers* books), 57 M22 units were actually built for 1965 production. The engineering change documentation for the M22 is dated December 12, 1964.

The change basically states that a new gearset is to be used with different synchronizer assemblies, the main case is to be modified to accept a drain plug, and the countershaft bore of the case is to be machined to accept a 1-inch-diameter countershaft. A letter to Zora Arkus-Duntov dated December 8, 1964, is referenced in this engineering change stating successful use of the M22 in Grand Sport Corvette field testing.

So exactly what is an M22? The RPO M22 stands for Heavy-Duty Close-Ratio. Many people think the gearset had some different alloy compared to the standard sets, but it didn't. According to original engineering drawings I have of the M22 first gear, it is made of an 8620-alloy steel. The same alloy is used to manufacture the M20 and M21 gears. The difference is the notation on the drawing to add shot peening to the gears.

Shot peening is a process in which the gear is blasted (like sand blasting) with steel shot. Steel shot

*This is a pair of Muncie first gears. The gear on the left is the standard M20 and M21 and the gear on the right is the M22. I placed them back-to-back so you can see the difference in the helix angles of the teeth. The M22 is straighter.*

is spherical and the gear surface develops thousands of microscopic dimples when the shot hits the gear. These dimples reduce stress risers on the area's gear teeth that can develop cracks because of fatigue.

The tooth counts and gear pressure angles of M20, M21, and M22 gears are the same. The difference is the helix angle. If you reduce the helix

angle of the gear you reduce thrust loading on the main case. Reduced thrust loading reduces heat and yields less horsepower loss to the rear wheels, but it increases gear noise. Hence the name "RockCrusher." Muncie 4-speeds have varying helix angles in the gearsets. Typically, the M20/M21 gearsets have a first-gear helix angle of 26.4 degrees and an input shaft angle of 39 degrees. The reduction in the angle with the M22 is quite substantial. The M22 first gear has an angle of 14.5 degrees and the input shaft is 24.2 degrees.

### 1966–1967

Several major improvements began in 1966. The diameter of the main case countershaft bore was officially increased to 1 inch. The most common main case casting was 3885010. This larger diameter was necessary because the big-block and small-block engines were producing more power. As a result, all M20, M21, and M22 countergears had to be redesigned to accommodate a larger countershaft. The needle bearings changed from .156 to .125 inch and the diameter of the spacer tubes also changed. New thrust washers

*The standard first-gear sleeve is on the top and the sleeve for the M22 is on the bottom (GM PN 3932228). It has flats ground into it to promote better oiling so that first gear does not seize to it. In road-racing applications, when you are in fourth gear doing more than 100 mph, first gear is spinning on the mainshaft at more that twice the mainshaft's RPM. This is one of those undocumented parts that is not listed in all the parts books but takes some digging to find. Later you could get a roller bearing M22 first-gear assembly directly from Chevrolet (GM PN 3965752). The roller first gear was designed to prevent gear seizures in high-speed road-race conditions.*

*The early 24-tooth maindrive is on the left and the later 1966–1970 model with 21 teeth is on the right. Reducing the number of teeth made a huge difference in reducing breakage of this gear; it becomes stronger while keeping the same gear diameter. This gave it a thicker tooth profile. I always use an apple pie as an analogy. A pie divided into four equal pieces obviously has larger pieces than the same pie divided into eight pieces.*

for the countergear were also needed because their bore size changed and the location of the holding tang of the thrust washer was also redesigned.

The synchronizer assemblies were also updated to what is commonly called a "shoulder style" synchro ring. The early 1963–1965 ring had a tendency to crack at the strut key slot. Therefore, the ring was redesigned with material added to create a shoulder in front of the synchro teeth. It's important to know that the later rings used a narrow synchronizer hub to compensate for this increased thickness. If you mix them up you end up with shifting problems.

The M20 gearset's front end was also redesigned to handle more power. Both the M20 input shaft and front of the countergear were machined with thicker teeth. This was accomplished by reducing the input shaft tooth count to 21 from 24 and the countergear's maindrive section to 25 from 29 teeth. The 25/21-tooth headset ratio is 1.19:1 and the 29/24 ratio is 1.21:1. This yields a slightly different M20 ratio set.

### Gear Ratios

**M20**
First, 2.52:1
Second, 1.88:1
Third, 1.46:1
Fourth, 1.0:1
Reverse, 2.59:1

**M21**
First, 2.20:1
Second, 1.64:1
Third, 1.28:1
Fourth, 1.0:1
Reverse, 2.27:1

**M22**
First, 2.20:1
Second, 1.64:1
Third, 1.28:1
Fourth, 1.0:1
Reverse, 2.27:1
(heavy duty)

## Available Gear Ratios

Prior to 1966 order options really didn't exist for Muncies. General Motors optioned cars with either the M20 or M21 ratios based on engine types and axle ratios. Many window and tank stickers exist from before 1966 that list cars as having M20s when in fact they had M21s. M22 production was rare in both 1966 and 1967; 29 were produced in 1966 and only 20 in L88 Corvettes in 1967.

Speedometer fitting placement was also changed. Before 1966 the speedometer gear "bullet" fitting on the extension housing was located on the driver's side in the middle of the shift linkage and below the oil level. The passenger-side speedometer extension housing also has added material between the upper shifter mounting holes. These extension housings always had a tendency to leak as well as get in the way of aftermarket shifters. For some reason, Pontiac kept the driver-side speedo while Chevrolet and Oldsmobile did not.

A small update was also added to the pivot pin on the sidecover that holds the whole internal interlock and detent system. It was press-fitted into the cover but it had a tendency to fall

*Webbing has been added to late-style extensions (casting PN 3857584). The passenger-side speedo tailhousing is always desired because it gets the driver-side speedo away from the linkage. Looking for the webbing is an easy way to recognize the casting when looking for parts.*

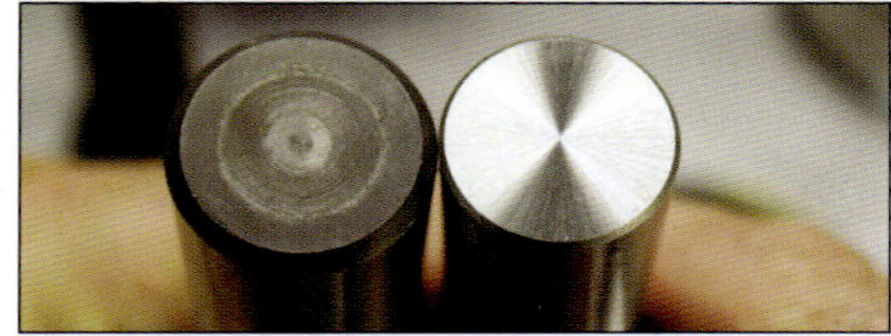

*The left countershaft is 1 inch in diameter and the right is 7/8 inch. Sometimes it's difficult to see the difference. A great way to restore and upgrade worn-out pre-1966 cases is to just bore them out to fit the later shafts and upgrade the gearset. The larger countershaft is needed to handle the load of big-block engines. The larger the shaft, the more surface area the case has to support it.*

*The 1963–1965 needle countergear needle bearing on the left is .156 inch in diameter. Four rows with 20 needles per row were used. The later design reduced the diameter of the needle to .125 inch because of the larger countershaft, which used four rows with 28 needles per row.*

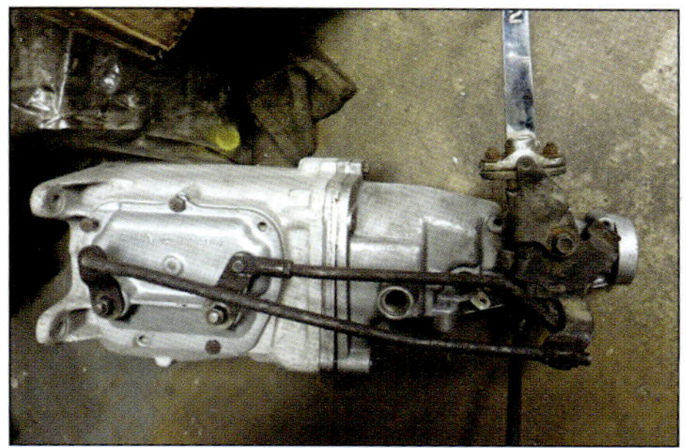

*This is essentially an original 1964 442 Oldsmobile Muncie casing with the original factory shifter. The sidecover pivot pin has no "hat" and can fall into the transmission. The speedometer fitting is located right where the linkage is. It's also below the oil level and prone to leaks. By 1966 it was relocated to the upper passenger side.*

*These are the two types of sidecover pivot pins that were used. Always use a later-style pin (right) when doing a rebuild. Some people simply pressed out the old pin and welded a blob of metal to the end of it.*

into the transmission. The new pin design simply added a hat to the end of the pin so it could not fall through.

Beginning in 1967, transmissions had a date designator added to the serial numbers. For prior years only a month and date were added.

### 1968, 1969 and 1970

The 1968 model was identical to the 1967 model except for a main case casting alloy change. The most common main case casting used during this period was 3925660. The front bearing retainer was also changed to a thicker casting. The height of the casting changed from

*If you are going to switch extension housings so that you can use a passenger-side speedometer fitting, you must make sure the mainshaft can accommodate the different position of the drivegear. The upper shaft has the single position for the driver's side and the lower shaft has more area added to the back for the passenger's side. The hole in the shaft was actually used on 1969–1970 models that had a clip-on plastic gear.*

*The late-style synchro hub and blocking rings (left) were used on 1966–1974 transmissions. Adding more material in front of the teeth reinforced the blocking rings. The hub had to be narrowed to make room for this additional material. The early hub and ring combination is on the right. Early hubs measured 1.150 inches across the spline face and later hubs measured 1.020 inches.*

roughly .325 inch to .450 inch. This made piloting the transmission into the bellhousing an easier operation.

More M22s were produced from 1968 to 1970 than in any other

*Notice the thicker shoulder of the later-style ring (left). The early ring (right) had a problem: Cracks developed at the key slot. Mixing early rings with a late hub causes excessive clearance and ring damage.*

period. Using data from Alan Colvin's *Chevrolet by the Numbers* books there were approximately 13,700 M22s made in the era compared to approximately 6,400 made in 1971 and 1972. What that means is that from 1968 to 1970 there were more factory 10-spline-input M22s assembled than the later 26-splines.

The 1969 design changes were subtle, and now all models had drain plugs as a standard issue. It was no longer just an M22 thing.

This was also the first year of "bolt-on" shifter shafts. Shifter shafts damaged because of broken studs or stripped threads were now a problem of the past. The rectangular drive portion of the shifter shaft was also increased in length from .605 to .722 inch. Shifter linkage arms were changed because the drive slot now had to be longer to match the drive portion of the mating shaft. The slot width of .315 inch remained unchanged. Putting a later linkage arm on a pre-1969 shaft can cause the linkage to become loose and out of alignment.

The speedometer drivegear only came as a molded 8-tooth gear. It was held in place with a spring-steel clip. It was obviously a move to save money and consolidate inventory since all transmissions would be assembled internally using all the same parts. Before 1969, different internal steel drivegears were installed to match specific axle ratios and tire sizes. The later plastic drivegears frequently failed; the transmission had to be disassembled and the equivalent press-on 8-tooth steel gear had to be used anyway.

Serial numbers from 1969 on were appended with a ratio designator. See Chapter 2 for more information on serial numbers.

The 1970 model was the same as the 1969, and 1970 proved to be a transitional year. The final main case casting of 3925661 was introduced, but there are huge overlaps in date codes. This means a transmission could be assembled in April with a 3925661 case and then in July with a 3925660 case.

The introduction of the transmission controlled spark (TCS) switch on the Muncie sidecover seemed to appear in 1970. This is an emissions device and its function is to disable the ignition system's vacuum advance until the transmission is shifted into fourth gear. Owners of most of these cars eliminated this system because they felt it hurt performance. It's quite common to see the switch plugged off or just filled with sealant.

### 1971–1974

In the final years of Muncie production, the best engineering

*This is a typical transmission controlled spark (TCS) sidecover. The switch is in great shape. Some switches have a bayonet end (shown), and later ones have a pin-type male connector.*

improvements for strength were incorporated into the gearboxes. The biggest change was the number of splines on both the input and output shafts. The input shaft spline count was increased from 10 to 26 splines along the same 1.125-inch-diameter shaft. The output shaft was increased from 27 splines to 32.

The 3925661 main case casting was used exclusively and a new tailhousing (3978764) with only three shifter-mounting holes was added. The transmission was also 3/4 inch longer than older models. Fitment issues might arise when installing one of these transmissions in a pre-1971 car. The shifter bolt pattern does not allow early linkage mounting plates to bolt to it. You have to shorten the driveshaft; of course, you also have to change the clutch disc and driveshaft yoke. Hurst Competition Plus shifters designed for earlier transmissions usually do not fit on these gearboxes. You have to purchase Hurst shifters intended for the make and model car that these gearboxes came in.

A few undocumented synchronizer updates were made. The design

*This photo shows that the overall length of the rectangular drive portion is longer on the bolt-style arm compared to that of the stud type. The rectangular slot of the linkage arm must fit properly. Mixing late long-slot arms on early short-slot shafts causes the linkage to go out of alignment.*

of the slider strut key groove was wider and tapered to reduce key wear. These assemblies came with heavier strut key springs. The synchronizer hubs had a very tight press fit to the mainshaft because the hubs apparently were nitrided. (Nitriding is a heat-treating process that adds surface hardness to the hub splines without distortion.) The sidecovers of some 1970 units had the heavier 20-pound detent spring but by 1971 all the covers had these springs.

All ratios (M20, M21, and M22) came with the 26/32-spline configuration. Even to this day there is a misconception that all "fine spline" Muncies are M22 "RockCrushers," which is not true. In actuality, more M20 units were produced with this configuration than were M21 and M22 models. The last year that the

*The left shifter shaft has a 3/8-24 threaded stud with machined flats on both sides. The 1969-and-up shafts used a bolt-on style, which eliminated broken studs and stripped threads.*

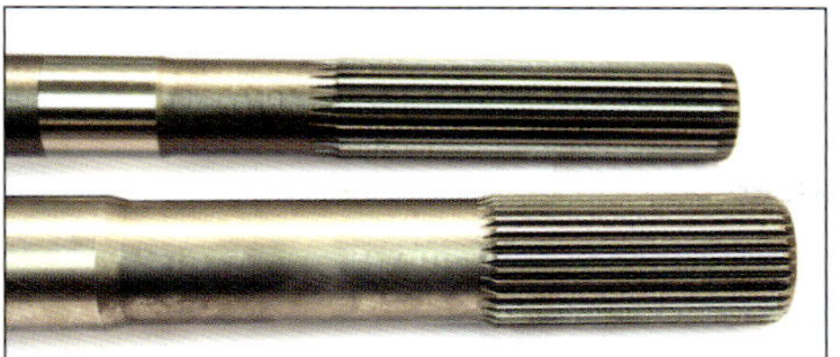

*The upper mainshaft has 27 splines and the lower has 32. Because larger-spline 1971–1974 Muncies are larger in diameter, a different driveshaft yoke is needed. The extension housings also take different bushings and seals. Make sure you order the proper gasket and seal kits when rebuilding these later units.*

*This synchro slider is the earlier design with the smaller strut key pocket. There are no part numbers in the GM system that differentiate these assemblies. Typically, the strut key springs had a lighter tension compared to later styles.*

M22 ratio was available as an option was 1972.

By the end of 1974, Muncies were no longer being installed in GM cars. The weaker BorgWarner ST10 replaced them and by 1975 big-block cars were no longer being produced. At this time, the Corvette had a 165-hp small-block engine, catalytic converter, and "unleaded fuel only" stickers on the gas cap doors. Transmissions had to be geared to work with economy axle ratios such as a 3.08:1 rear. The Muncie was never designed for that. To redesign the Muncie and downgrade it would have cost a lot of money. It was much easier to replace it with the ST10. The ST10 duplicated the current spline configuration, length, and shifter bolt patterns.

The glory days of the 4-speed Muncie were over and BorgWarner once again was back in the saddle. The ST10's production in GM vehicles was from 1974 to 1988. Because of production quality issues, no Corvettes were produced in 1983. The ST10 was used with an overdrive in 1984 to 1988 Corvettes only and was called the Doug Nash 4+3 (even though the patent for the original Muncie includes the ST10). In a sense, 1988 marked the last year this type of transmission was used in a GM vehicle.

*The later slider had a smoother, ramped, strut key pocket. These used a heaver tension spring compared to earlier sliders. Today I use a spring that has a tension between the early and late springs.*

*Notice the difference in the drive slots of these arms. The example on the left is for pre-1969 transmissions and the one on the right is for those that accept a 3/8-16 threaded bolt. The slot on later arms always has a circular cutout to make room for the bolt. Adapter clips are available to take up the extra space so you can use later arms on stud-type shifter shafts.*

*The left synchro hub is the standard hub and the right is a factory-nitrided hub. Notice the color difference between them. These hubs fit extremely tightly on mainshafts, and you need to have the proper press clamps or pullers to remove them.*

# MUNCIE 4-SPEED IDENTIFICATION

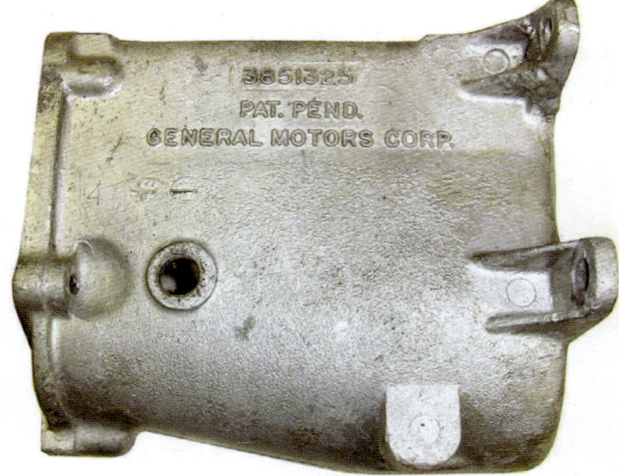

*This is the standard Muncie 4-speed case. It has a seven-digit serial number cast into the case on the passenger's side. These are usually the first numbers used to start the identification process.*

*This is Brian Higgins of the SK Tranny Shop. Shops like this are a great place to research castings and part numbers. Few people today will ever be able to amass this number of Muncie parts.*

It was much easier to stockpile Muncie spare parts and cores in the 1970s than it is today. Reliable sources to validate information regarding serial and casting numbers will get scarcer as time passes. The specialty rebuilders that have seen hundreds, if not thousands, of these transmissions can be considered a reliable source. These guys stockpiled a lot of parts! I've met many of these rebuilders and have had the pleasure to create great friendships with them. I spent a great deal of time sorting through their parts. The guy who

may know how to rebuild one, yet sees only two transmissions a year, is probably not a reliable source. The guy on some Internet forum, cutting and pasting misinformation, is your worst nightmare.

Several times a day I'm asked, by email or phone, how to identify a Muncie. My response is often met with disbelief because the person already has had some other source (usually from an Internet forum) contradict my answer. Some people don't even have a Muncie. They often get angry because they don't

want to face up to the fact that they got burned and made a bad 4-speed purchase.

Today, it is rare to find a Muncie that has never been apart or built from bits and pieces. Untouched "survivor" Muncies are rare; so are the ones that have correct correlating casting and serial numbers.

Main cases often suffered from broken mounting ears, but the later cases had thicker, stronger mounting ears. Its quite common to see later cases replace early ones for this reason. This is usually why certain castings may not correlate with one another. Tailhousings often get damaged where the reverse shifter shaft lock pin sits, and at both the shifter and main mount bolt-boss locations.

Because date-coded serial numbers and VINs were only stamped (not cast) into the main case, the main case should be your starting point. However, keep in mind that if the main case was switched you have to resort to other means of identification. You can think of them as a system of checks and balances.

Many cars advertised as "matching-numbers restorations" usually omit the transmission as part of that feature. I created a Facebook page at www.MuncieBook.com. This page is in place to support this book and it's free. Feel free to upload pictures and ask questions. Some of the best Muncie builders participate on that page.

## Muncie RPO Codes

Just three types of Muncie 4-speeds are available based on the RPO (regular production option) code used when a car was ordered: the M20 (standard wide-ratio), M21 (close-ratio), and M22 (heavy-duty close-ratio). (The M does not stand for "Muncie.")

Typically, when you ordered a GM car you had standard options and accessories installed. "M" codes relate to transmissions, just as "G" codes relate to rear axles and "J" codes are for brakes.

| Manufacturer's Suggested Retail Price: (Includes Federal Excise Tax & Suggested Dealer Delivery & Handling Charge) | | |
|---|---|---|
| **Model:** 19437  CORVETTE SPT COUPE | 4875 | 00 |
| Destination Charge | 126 | 00 |
| Subtotal | 5001 | 00 |
| Manufacturer's Suggested Retail Delivered Prices on Options and Accessories installed on this Vehicle by the Manufacturer | | |
| 2986AA  SILVER PEARL | | 00 |
| 2J50MA  VACUUM POWER BRAKE | 46 | 15 |
| 2M21AA  4 SPD CL RATIO TRAN | 202 | 35 |
| 2A01BA  TINTED GLASS | 16 | 80 |
| 2A31AA  POWER WINDOWS | 63 | 95 |
| 2U69AC  PB AM/FM RADIO | 189 | 75 |
| 2K66DA  TRANSISTOR IGN EQ | 80 | 75 |
| 2N14AB  SIDE DUAL EXHAUST | 144 | 65 |
| 2F41AC  SPL SUSPENSION EQ | 39 | 90 |
| 2G81NA  POSITRACT AXLE 370R | 46 | 15 |
| 2L71AA  435 HP V8 TURBOJET | 480 | 10 |

*This 1967 Corvette has a build sheet with an RPO code for an M21 close-ratio 4-speed. Notice the other letters and the type of options they represent. Because M21 is just a code, later Corvettes or other 4-speed cars didn't have Muncies; those equipped with a Super T10 4-speed could have an M21 or an M20 code. Window and tank sticker resources reveal that there was never an M21 option printed on a sticker before 1966, even though many M21s existed I believe the final-drive ratio determined whether a close- or wide-ratio transmission was installed.*

**Muncie Gear Ratios Based on RPO Code**

| Code | Type (:1) | Years |
|---|---|---|
| M20 | Wide-Ratio, 2.56/1.91/1.48/1.00/3.16 | 1963–1965 |
| M20 | Wide-Ratio, 2.52/1.88/1.46/1.00/3.11 | 1966–1974 |
| M21 | Close-Ratio, 2.20/1.64/1.28/1.00/2.27 | 1963–1974 |
| M22 | Heavy-Duty Close-Ratio, 2.20/1.64/1.28/1.00/2.27 | 1965–1972 |

## Main Case Casting Numbers

Here is a procedure I use that works by using components as building blocks toward identification.

The patent that was originally filed on November 29, 1957, for the T10/Muncie design was approved 5½ years later on May 7, 1963. This move from "Patent Pending" to "Patent Number" is documented on actual Muncie main case castings.

The evolution of case design also helps pinpoint the year a case was released. The main case casting number was used for either a specific year or series of years. Casting numbers are not GM part numbers. Some cases may look identical and have a different casting number but have the same GM part number. Usually a casting number is changed because of a design change. This could be an alloy improvement, a casting tool change, or some physical change.

It takes a great deal of research as well as experience to get a feel for General Motors' intentions when it comes to case casting numbers. Most of the books and articles I have seen, combined with some bits of Internet folklore, tend to have the same flaws because most information is copied and simply edited and resubmitted. I have done my own research by looking at literally thousands of cases, extensions, and sidecovers to draw my own conclusions. I can guarantee that most people reading this book

will never see some of the items I've stumbled across.

Muncie 4-speeds pretty much have a solid chronological order regarding the main case, retainer, midplate, and extension housing casting numbers. Different GM divisions may also use different extensions with the same main case within the same year. Casting number revisions are always chronological, which means that a higher number corresponds to a later part.

People often get confused about what a casting number is. Simply put, it is the number that is actually cast into the case when the molten aluminum is poured into the case mold. (A serial number is stamped into the case by hand, usually with numbered and lettered punches.) As a mold is poured, date-coded clocks are cast into most cases that represent the month, week, and sometimes day the case was cast. These casting dates or "clocks" are not generally necessary to determine what type of Muncie you have. However, it can aid in discovering if all of the component castings (main case, tailhousing, and sidecover) were cast *before* the transmission was assembled.

## Serial Numbers

Serial numbers are stamped into the case. It is a date code for when the transmission was assembled based on the model year, not calendar year.

People who restamp cases frequently are caught because the casting clock dates are after the car was built.

Serial numbers for Muncie 4-speeds always begin with the letter "P," which stands for Muncie Plant (not "passenger car.") "M" and "N" were used to identify 3-speed Muncies; "O" identifies the Saginaw 3-speed with overdrive.

Serial numbers from 1963 to 1966 included only the month and day. For example, P0101 indicates January 1. From 1967 to 1968, the serial number used year, month, and day designators; the month designator is now a letter. For example, the serial number P8A01 is January 1, 1968.

If you have a Muncie dated with a December build date it was actually built the previous year. An example is the date code P8T13. This is for a 1968 production car. The "T" stands for December and 13 is the day.

To confirm this simply look at the VIN. It usually begins with 18S101350 or 28N12950. This means the Muncie was assembled December 13, 1967, for the 1968 model year. The VIN is usually a low number because it was

*Date code format for 1963–1966 model years was just a month and day. Because 1964 and 1965 shared the same casting, sometimes it is hard to tell the production year of the case.*

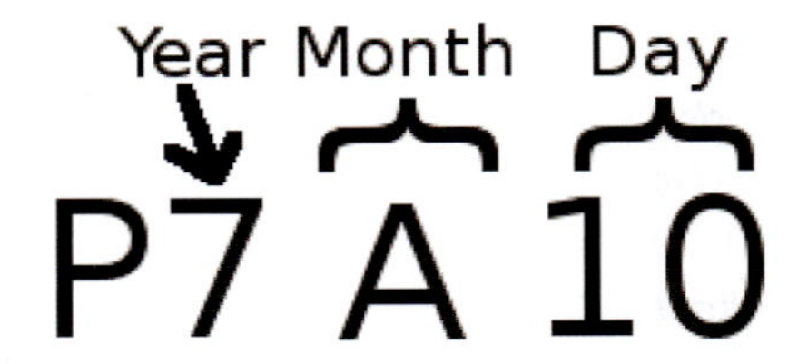

*The 1967 and 1968 vehicles received a year, month, and day designator. Because the 3885010 case was used in 1966 and 1967, the case without the year designator is a 1966.*

actually going into an early 1968 car.

The 1969–1974 Muncies received a ratio designator at the end of the serial number: "A" for M20, "B" for M21, "C" for M22. An example is P2D23B. This is April 23, 1972, M21

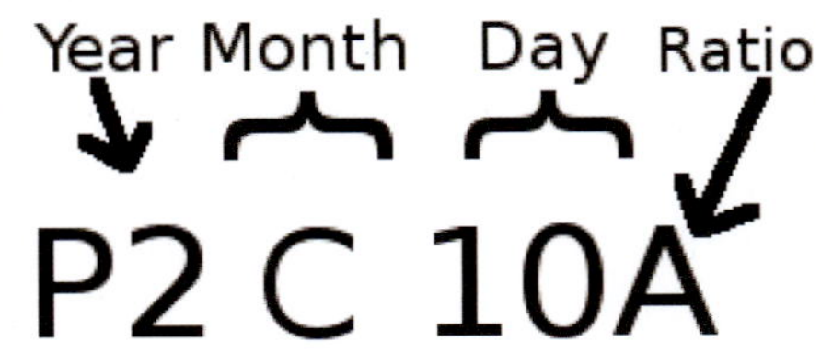

*The 1969–1974s received a year, month, day, and ratio designator. Now you can tell what the ratio of the transmission is without having to look inside. It's still a good habit to double-check the gears to confirm the ratio because often the ratios were switched around.*

ratio. It's also not uncommon to see double stamps or sometimes even double letters at the end.

## Main Cases

Let's take a look at how the Muncie main case evolved from 1963 to 1974.

### 1963

The first Muncie case was number 3831704. It had a 7/8-inch counter-shaft bore and used a 6207-type

## Assembly Month Code

These letters are used to represent a Muncie's month of assembly.

| | |
|---|---|
| A | January |
| B | February |
| C | March |
| D | April |
| E | May |
| H | June |
| K | July |
| M | August |
| P | September |
| R | October |
| S | November |
| T | December |

## Main Case Castings

| Code | Year | Notes |
|---|---|---|
| 3831704 | 1963 | Only small 6207NR front bearing; Patent Pending; 7/8-inch bore |
| 3839606 | 1963–1964 | Regular bearing; Patent Pending; 7/8-inch bore |
| 3851325 | 1964–1965 | Mostly 1964; Patent Pending; 7/8-inch bore |
| 3851325 | 1964–1965 | Patent Number; 7/8-inch bore |
| 3864848 | 1965 | Patent Number; 7/8-inch bore |
| 3864____ | 1965 | Milled off last 3 digits; Patent Number; 7/8-inch bore |
| 3885010 | 1966–1967 | Patent Number; 1-inch bore |
| 3925660 | 1968–1970 | Patent Number; 1-inch bore |
| 3925661 | 1969–1974 (some early 1975 cars) | Patent Number; 1-inch bore |

front bearing. All ball bearings have standardized numbers used by the bearing industry. The 6207 bearing's dimensions are 35-mm bore, 72-mm outside diameter, and 17-mm width.

The Muncie case (3831704) replaced the T10 4-speed in the 1963 Chevrolet Bel Air and Corvette by mid-May of that year. The T10 front bearing size was reduced in diameter in 1963 only. This meant that the transmission's front bearing retainer and register bore of the bellhousing were also smaller in diameter. The smaller 6207-type bearing replaced the larger 6307 bearing in 1963.

The first Muncie copied the smaller bearing and retainer combination of the T10. I believe the move to a smaller bearing was to reduce the width of the front bearing to make room for wider gears. By 1963, wider gears improved the T10; this meant that the front bearing had to get narrow to compensate for the size difference of the front portion of the countergear.

The 6307N bearing has a 35-mm bore, an 80-mm outside diameter, and is 21 mm thick.

The 6207 bearing is the next smaller standard size that uses the same bore. However, it is thinner by 4 mm and smaller in diameter by 8 mm. Because the Muncie was really GM's design improvement of the T10, the 7/8-inch-diameter countershaft was also used in 1963.

By late 1963 the rare 3839606 case started to show up in cars with a larger bearing bore. The fact is General Motors couldn't use a standard 6307-style bearing with a width of 21 mm because the gears were already tooled and made. Therefore, they kept the width of the smaller 6207-style bearing of 17 mm but went with the standard outside diameter

*This is the 1963-only 3831704 main case with "PAT. PEND." cast above "General Motors Corp." Notice that the drain plug boss was not drilled out. The casting clock codes are at right above the fill plug. The clock looks like a mathematical fraction with a 1/2-inch circle around it; they were a way to track any quality-control issues. The number represents the month and the dots represent the week. Most of the time the other clock is blank, but occasionally it represents numbers and deviations to the original blueprint. Later cases seem to only have one clock. A "4" next to the casting is the mold pattern number.*

of a 6307. This is called a narrow 6307 bearing (PN N307LOE).

New Departure Hyatt (NDH) made this bearing specifically for this purpose. Their number was 41307B. It is unique to the Muncie and was used until the very end of production in all main cases with the exception of the 3831704 case.

### 1964 and 1965

By 1964 the 3851325 case appeared. Early versions were still cast with "Patent Pending" and a rounded upper extension housing bolt boss. By late 1964 the 3851325 case was cast with GM Patent Number 3088336. The 1965 case with the same casting number has a squared-off upper extension housing boss.

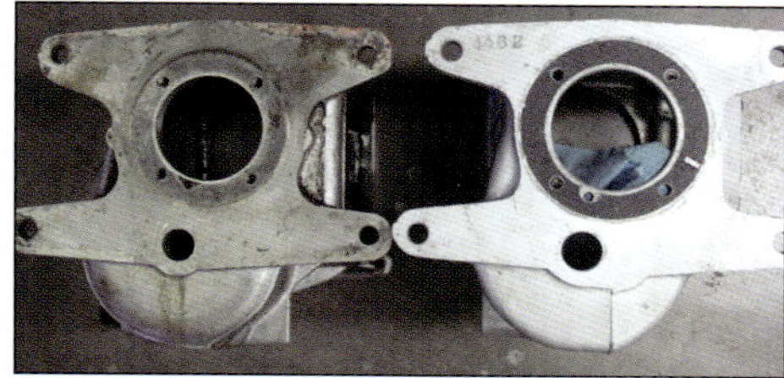

*The left case is a 1963 T-10. The bearing bore is smaller than the Muncie case on the right. The 3831704 case used the same bore as the 1963 T10.*

*The 3839609 main case was used during 1963 and 1964. It's identical to the 3831704, except it had a bigger front bearing bore. Most of these castings look very rough. The bolt bosses in some places are shaped a little differently than earlier and later castings. It may have been from a different foundry. These surface from time to time but are rare.*

Corvette production determined how Muncie design evolved. By late 1965, the 396 Turbo Jet engine, rated at 425 hp, was introduced. A very small number of 396 engines also found their way into the 1965 Impala. I learned from speaking to many builders that the rare 3864848 case seems to be in a few Corvettes and full-size GM cars with big-block engines. The 3864848 case with the last 848 numbers milled off is in some full-size cars, such as the Impala. This usually indicates that the gears used in the milled cases might be of a different steel alloy. The case appears to be identical to a 3851325 case so perhaps it is made of a different aluminum alloy. It appears that more milled cases are in circulation compared to unmilled cases. They all seem to come from big-block cars.

### 1966 and 1967

The 1966 main cases saw some additional design changes. With the introduction of the 3885010 case, the countershaft bore was increased to 1 inch. The case countershaft bore usually stretched out so the increase in shaft diameter spread the countershaft load over a wider area.

This case was used to the end of

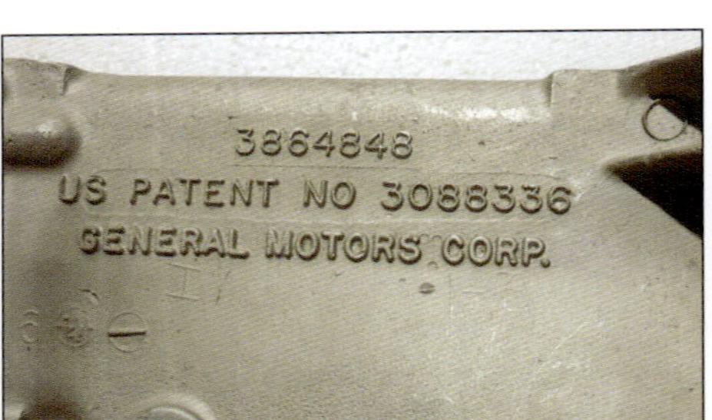

*The 3864848 case, with a December 17, 1964, build date, was probably for an early 1965 car. These cases were run in conjunction with the 3851325 case. This might have been a different alloy because its appearance is identical to the 3851325 case and it was to be used strictly with the new big-block 396 engine. (Photo Courtesy Ed Hartnett)*

*The early "3851325 PAT. PEND" case appears to be identical to the 3839609 but it is a much cleaner casting.*

*These two milled 3864 cases have March 1965 assembly dates. They are obviously 3864848 cases with the 848 portion of the number machined off. (Coincidentally, March 1965 seems to be a time when the 396 engine started to migrate into more vehicles, such as Z16 Chevelles, Corvettes, and full-size Impalas.) These transmissions probably were assembled with special alloy gears, because the case casting is identical to the 3851325 as well. Usually when an external modification is made to the case, such as milling, it means a special internal mod. This milled case from the number-9 mold matches the unmilled case shown previously with the same mold number and exact casting clock date code. What you can see is that before March 1965 these cases were not milled. (Photo Courtesy Ed Hartnett)*

*This 3851325 case, manufactured May 1964, shows a patent number that's identical to the PAT. PEND. case. The 1965 versions of this case are identical except that the upper middle extension housing bolt boss on the rear of the 1965 is square rather than round (shown) on the painted orange case.*

*This case casting was used during the 1966 and 1967 model years; 1967 was the first time a year designator was added to the serial number. This one has a January 19, 1967, date code.*

*This is a 1967 3885010 case dated June 2, 1967. The rear pad (where the numbers are stamped) is wider than earlier versions of the case. The mounting ears also have thicker gussets than earlier cases. This casting design evolved into the 1968-and-up castings.*

*This 1968 3925660 main case has a P8R04 assembly date and was cast in a number-2 mold. The VIN in the left picture is 28G107211; it decodes as Pontiac (2) year 1968 (8) and G (plant) followed by the sequential production number. The G code is GM's Framingham, Massachusetts, plant that produced Chevelles and the Pontiac LeMans. Therefore, this is a LeMans case.*

1967. Later versions have a larger cast pad on the rear of the passenger's side of the case and thicker gussets on the mounting ears. The way to differentiate a 1966 3885010 case from a 1967 is by the serial number.

### 1968 and 1970

The 3925660 cases were used primarily in 1968 to 1970. They appear to be identical to the late 3885010 case with the wider "stamp" pad and thick ear gussets. Some spots also have more material and the case has a thicker look to it. Perhaps an alloy change as well as a tooling change warranted a new number.

By the start of 1969 these cases and all future cases had the drain plug boss drilled and threaded. The 3925661 casting seemed to surface by the last quarter of 1969. Stamped serial numbers for all 1969 model year cases also included the year designator.

### 1970 to 1974

The last Muncie case was the 3925661. The "661" is considered the strongest factory GM case. It is

*Here is a rare 3925661 casting from a 1969 Camaro. The assembly date of P9P16A translates to September 16, 1969. The "A" stands for M20. Notice the odd casting clock above the fill plug and that it was drilled for a drain plug. This was mold pattern number 1.*

identical to the 3925660 case but definitely has a different color. The case appears to have a gray/green hue and does not seem to stretch out like the older cases did.

It was used primarily with the 26-spline input shaft and larger 32-spline output-shaft models, so it appears that they were looking to optimize strength everywhere possible since the 454 engine was introduced in 1970. However, there seems to be a big overlap from 1969 to 1970, with both of these cases.

*This is a 3925661 case from a 1974 Corvette M20 transmission. It has an August 7, 1974, build date. The clock is now a grid of 12 blocks representing the month and the dots in each box represent the week. This one was cast in the fourth week of January 1974 in mold number 15.*

*This is a 1970 M20 case. The VIN is hard to read. This is mold number 1. Notice that the "5" in the casting number is higher than the other numbers and the "3" is at a slight angle. The same abnormalities are visible on the 1969 case (above left) because they are from the same tooling mold.*

## Service Cases and Transmissions

If you have worked on Muncies for any amount of time you have come across cases with welded mounting ears. These cases were obviously repaired but sometimes a replacement case was the only fix. The casting number depends on the date the service case was installed. The replacement case (GM PN 3925659) was used for all 1966–1974 Muncies as listed in the GM AC DELCO 1978 service parts manual. It was a 3925661 casting.

If you have to replace an early 7/8-inch case, a later casting is offered with the thick ears but machined for the early shaft. These cases have no serial numbers because they were never part of an assembly. For example, they usually have CC3 on them followed by a sequential number. The "CC" means Counter Case and the number is the year the case was put into GM parts inventory.

A CT3 is a replacement transmission. Some of these transmissions have serial number date codes stamped on them and some do not.

## Extension Housings and Sidecovers

Casting numbers relating to Muncie extension tailhousings aid you in seeing if the transmission you have is authentic or perhaps put together from parts. Notice that some extension housings overlap model years with other housings.

The reason for the overlap is simple. Certain make and model GM cars used one type while other models used something different. For example, the 3846429 was used in the Pontiac Tempest/GTO model

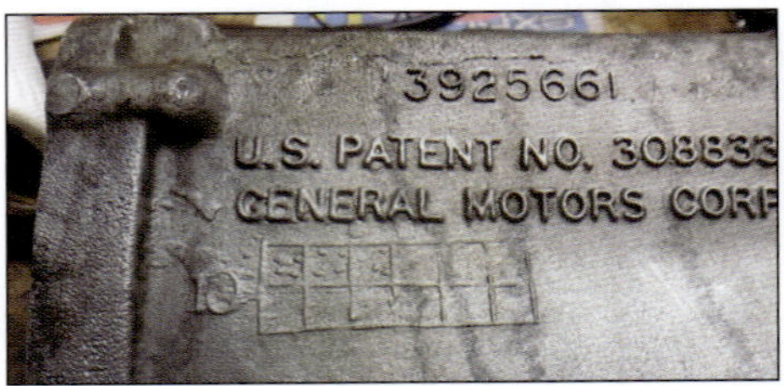

*This 3925661 case has a CC3 number of 42198. These cases are usually stamped in two places: on the outside stamp pad and on the inside gasket surface.*

platform from 1964 to 1970, yet the Firebird used the 3857584 casting from 1967 to 1970.

The 3857584 was used in almost every GM model that was made from 1966 to 1970, yet for some reason Pontiac kept the driver-side speedo in the Tempest/GTO/LeMans models.

Sidecovers are often swapped simply because it is easy to do. Basically, some covers were issued with stud-type shifter shafts and others with bolt-on shifter shafts. The TCS switch covers were sometimes plugged, unmachined, or had the switch installed. Switches can have rounded- or spade-shaped male connectors. Its rare to find a TCS cover with a switch that actually works or hasn't had the connector broken off.

*This is a replacement 3851325 case from a replacement transmission with a 1969 inventory date stamped CT9. The case has several unusual features. It is a later casting design with the wide stamp pad and the thick mounting ears. However, the 1964–1965 3851325 casting number was kept, as was the 7/8-inch countershaft bore. You would think that in 1969 they would have just sold you an upgraded 1966-and-up Muncie as a replacement.*

## Extension Tailhousing Identification

| Serial Number | Year | Description |
| --- | --- | --- |
| 3831731 | 1963 | Thin-fin tail; driver-side speedo; 27-spline |
| 3846429 | 1963 | Thin-fin tail; driver-side speedo; 27-spline |
| 3846429 | 1964–1965 | Regular, thick lower web; driver-side speedo; 27-spline (used up to 1970 in some Pontiac models) |
| 384362 | 1963–1964 | Long-tail; driver-side speedo; 27-spline (rare) |
| 9779246 | 1964–1965 | Pontiac Catalina long-tail; passenger-side speedo; 27-spline |
| 3857584 | 1966–1970 | Passenger-side speedo; 27-spline |
| 3978764 | 1970–1974 | Passenger-side speedo, 32-spline output |

Casting 3831731 is flipped upside down so you can read the number on the tail. Notice the lower "thin" fin.

Casting 3846429 is a wide-fin casting. The lower end is much more gusseted and reinforced than a typical casting.

Casting 3846429 is a thin-fin version of the 3846429 casting. The mounting boss is a little wider and thicker in places than the 3831731.

Casting 3857584 is pretty much identical to the wide-fin 3846429 tail. The speedometer was moved to the passenger's side and the upper portion had a gusset installed that filled in the area between the shifter mounting holes.

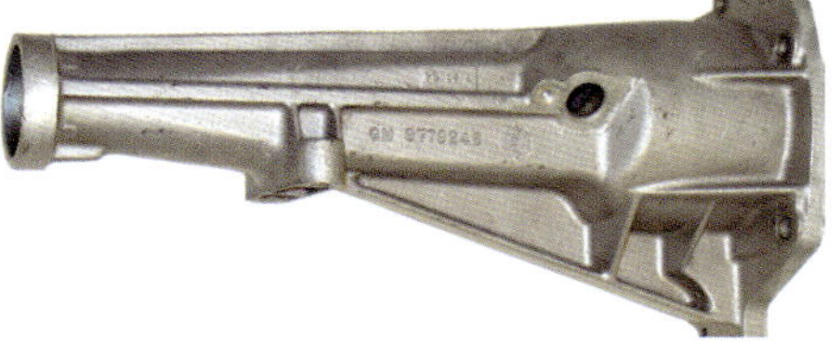

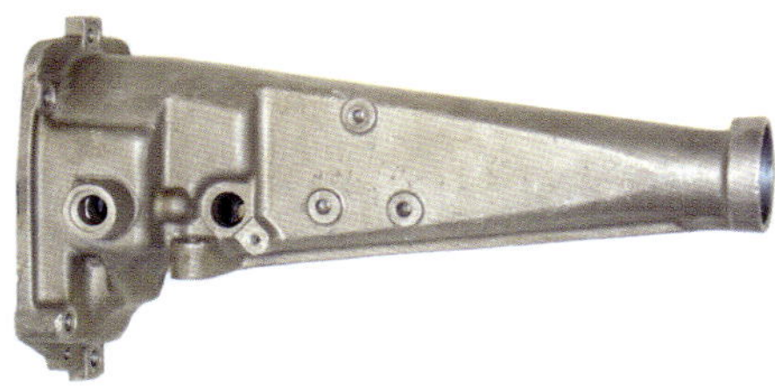

Casting 384362 is the long-tail version with a driver-side speedo. It duplicates the short extension mounting and shifter locations. This one is very rare. (Photo Courtesy Eric Davidson)

This casting number is followed by an "AA" marker after the serial number, but I have not determined what that marker meant. (Photo Courtesy Eric Davidson)

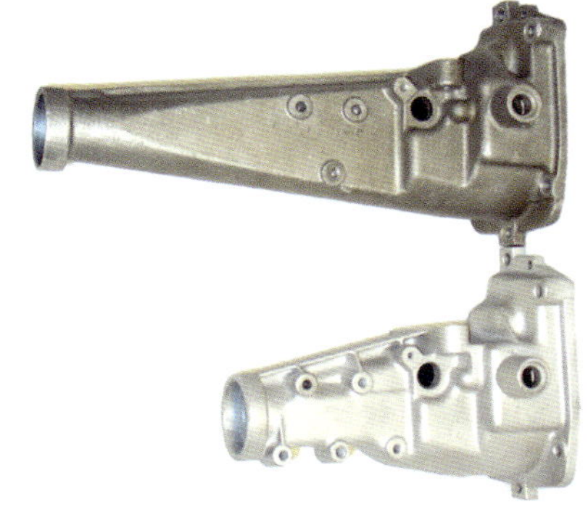

The long-tail casing 384362 (top) is basically an extended version of the 3846429 short driver-side speedometer tail (bottom). These early long tails were sand-cast. (Photo Courtesy Eric Davidson)

Casting 9779246 is a typical Catalina long-tail. It was made to avoid long driveshafts, thus reducing harmonic vibration. This is a rare Winters Foundry sand-cast piece. (Photo Courtesy Eric Davidson)

*This is a close-up of the Winters Foundry logo with a casting date of July 27, 1964. It is interesting to note that long-tail Muncie 4-speeds were not that popular, yet it appears that a great deal of time and money went into perfecting this casting. (Photo Courtesy Eric Davidson)*

*This is the die-cast version of the long-tail. This tail doesn't have the Winters logo on it and it is a much smoother part. Tooling up for a die casting is very expensive. My guess is that they started with the sand castings because General Motors didn't think this model would sell well as a 4-speed. Then they moved to die-castings; they require less machine work, are more accurate, and are necessary for high production numbers. (Photo Courtesy Eric Davidson)*

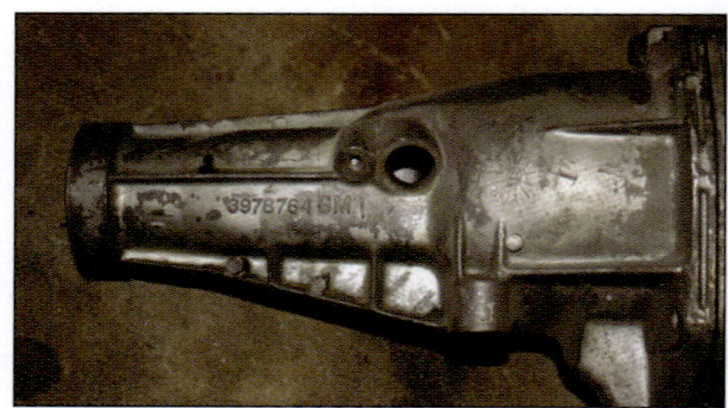

*Casting 3978764 is a later 32-spline mainshaft tail. It only has one bolt pattern for the shifter. (Photo Courtesy Eric Davidson)*



| Serial Number | Description |
| --- | --- |
| 3831707 | 1963–1966 Early sidecover stud shifter shafts |
| 3884685 | Cover issued with "584" tail stud shifter shafts |
| 3950306 | Short-boss with bolt-on shifter shafts, no switches |
| 3952642 | Long-boss bolt-on with TCS switch on 3-4 |
| 3952648 | Short-boss bolt-on with TCS switch on 3-4 (some have a boss for the switch that is cast but not machined on 3-4) |
| 335308 | Long-boss bolt-on with neutral safety switch and TCS switch (some have a boss for the switch that is cast but not machined on 1-2) |

*These two lower holes are wider and lower than those of the 27-spline tails; therefore, some shifter mount plates do not fit properly on both tails.*

*This is a typical 3831707 cast cover. It has the early non-hat-style pivot pin.*

*This cover has the better hat-style pivot pin. Early pins were prone to falling into the transmission. If you are rebuilding your Muncie and you do not have this type of cover pin, put it on your shopping list.*

*The 3884685 cover is a direct duplicate of the 3831707. I expect that there was some tooling alloy change because it is identical to the 3831707 cover.*

*The 3950306 cover was the first one used with bolt-on-style shifter shafts. This was the last cover that used a thin perimeter casting surrounding the upper middle bolt.*

*The 3952642 casting is more rare than most covers. It was the first long-boss cover and it had six pry tabs. This cover provided an improved radius to the upper bolt-hole surround.*

*This comparison shows a long-boss cover (left) and a short-boss cover (right). The long version has a better-defined gusset as well as a pry tab.*

*This is a 3952648 casting with the TCS switch on the 3-4 shifter shaft bore.*

*This is the second generation of plate casting 3831752. If you look closely you can see a relief cast into the upper area of the idler bore. This is because material was added around the rear-bearing bore.*

*This cover has an unmachined switch area found only in some 1969 models.*

## Midplate Castings

The casting number for the midplate never changed. Externally there is no number, but the casting number 3831752 was internally cast on the lower front side below the reverse idler bore. Two types of these midplates were cast. The 1963 plate had more material surrounding the reverse idler bore. This was eliminated after 1963.

*This is the first version of the 3831752 cast midplate. This early type is only found in 1963 transmissions. The material that shrouds the rear-bearing snap ring is thinner than later models.*

## Ratio Identification

As mentioned previously, we know that the Muncie came with several ratios. Because main cases are often swapped rather than being repaired, the best way to determine if you have an M20, M21, or M22 is to simply look at the gears.

Without removing the sidecover you can look at the input shaft and check for identification grooves cut into the spline. The "ID" groove system was good until several things changed. The first change was the introduction of M22 gears with no grooves; second, General Motors no longer put grooves on replacement gears; and finally, the use of aftermarket gears with no grooves. Here are three rules that will help you determine which transmission you have:

- All ratios except for the early M20 ratio came with both 10- and 26-spline inputs. The early M20 with the 24-tooth input only came in 10-spline.
- Muncies with 26-spline inputs and 32-spline output shafts came as M20, M21, and M22 transmissions.
- Before 1969, only M22 transmissions had drain plugs. From 1969 to 1974 all-ratio Muncies came with drain plugs.

Muncie countergears had the same number of teeth on first-, second-, and third-speed sections.

| Countergear Teeth | |
| --- | --- |
| **Transmission** | **Tooth Count** |
| Early M20 | 29, 22, 19, 17 |
| Late M20 | 25, 22, 19, 17 |
| M21/M22 | 27, 22, 19, 17 |

*The progression of the 10-spline input identification groove system. From left to right, early M20, M21, later M20, and M22. You really cannot get the early M20 and M22 mixed up because the early M20 came with a 7/8-inch countershaft, while the M22 did not.*

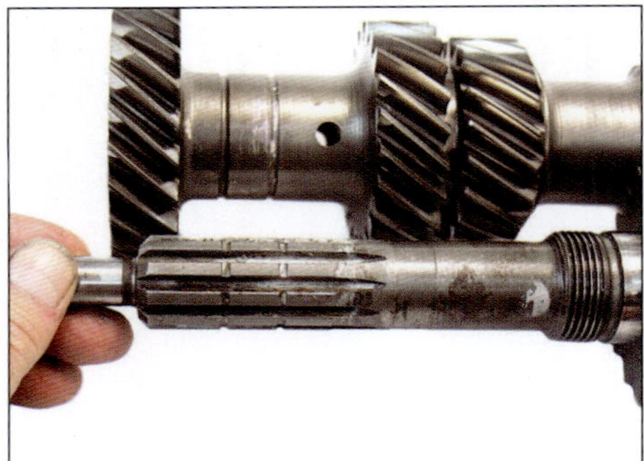

*This is an M20 two-groove input and matching two-groove countergear. The identification grooves were also a quick way for assembly-line workers to identify and install matching gearsets.*

*Here are three countergears: late M20 (top), M21 (middle), M22 (bottom). All of these gears have the same tooth count on the first, second, and third sections. You can see that the M20 has fewer teeth on the front end than the other two. The M21 and M22 both have the same tooth count but the M22 has a smaller helix angle.*

*Here are some 26-spline input shafts. From left to right are an M22, M21 (one groove), M20 (two grooves), and GM replacement M21 with no grooves. This is a good example of why looking at grooves on input shafts may not be a sure method of identification. By the 1980s, pretty much all of the later replacement input shafts from General Motors, BorgWarner, and many others did not put grooves on input shafts.*

In fact all of the upper-speed gears have the same tooth count regardless of ratios. Every first gear has 36 teeth, second gear has 30 teeth, and third gear has 27 teeth.

So how did the ratios change? A gear ratio is a combination of two ratios multiplied together. By changing the ratio of just the head set (input shaft and front of the countergear) you can change the overall ratio. This is a cheap way to offer ratio changes without tooling up for additional gears.

The mathematical formula for determining a gear ratio in these transmissions is:

$$\text{Ratio} = (A \div B) \times (C \div D)$$

Where:

A = headset-driven-gear (countergear front gear) tooth count
B = input-shaft tooth count
C = first-speed-gear tooth count
D = countergear tooth count

Let's use the late M20 and plug the tooth counts into the above formula. The headset-driven gear is the countergear front gear with a tooth count of 25. It is driven by the input shaft with 21 teeth. The countergear has 17 teeth on its first-gear section driving the actual first-speed gear with 36 teeth. Plug the tooth counts into the above formula and you get a first-gear ratio of 2.52:1.

$$(25 \div 21) \times (36 \div 17)$$
$$(1.190 \times 2.117)$$
$$2.52$$

*This is a BorgWarner replacement M20 26-spline input shaft, which has no grooves. Notice their circled "W" logo. Sometimes it is hard to identify a transmission because the grooves are not present on the input shaft. Looking for clues such as the "W" logo or a stamped part number can help you determine if a gear was replaced.*

## Hardware and Tags

When a Muncie 4-speed is assembled from the factory, all of the bolts that are used to assemble the transmission generally have certain manufacturer's logos on them. The seven bolts on the sidecover have the same logo. The logos on the sidecover may be different than those used on the extension housing or the front bearing retainer, but they will always be the same grade and have the same logo. If your bolt logos match and your front retainer locking tabs are in place it usually is a good indicator that the transmission has never been taken apart.

### Muncie Fasteners and Torque Specifications

| Description | Quantity | Size (inches) | Torque Value (ft-lbs) |
| --- | --- | --- | --- |
| Maindrive retainer | 4 | 3/8-16 x 1 | 25 |
| Sidecover | 7 | 5/16-18 x 3/4 | 18 |
| Extension housing | 3 | 3/8-16 x 1¾ | 25 |
| Extension housing | 2 | 7/16-14 x 1⅞ | 25 |
| Extension housing | 1 | 7/16-14 x 2½ | 25 |
| Fill plug | 1 | 1/2 NPT | 25 |
| Drain plug | 1 | 1/2 NPT | 25 |
| Speedo hold down | 1 | 1/4-20 x 5/8 | 10 |

*Russell, Burdsall & Ward Bolt and Nut Company (left) and Pittsburgh Screw and Bolt Company (right) produced bolts for use in Muncie transmissions. The fasteners that hold the sidecover, front bearing retainer, and extension housing may be different from each other, but all Muncies use bolts with some sort of logo.*

*Many rebuilders have bins full of tags. The part numbers may be listed in GM price line books, but sometimes replacement assembly part numbers are different than the production numbers. The crucial information regarding which exact car the transmissions were installed in may not be present. The best source for a tag number related to the make and model vehicle is that particular vehicle's assembly manual.*

Of course, every company has a unique logo on its bolts. "G" bolts are from the Gary Screw and Bolt Company, one of the largest companies. "SBC" bolts are from Standard Bolt, "NAT" bolts are from National Bolt and Nut Company, Towne Robinson Fastener manufactured "TR" bolts, and the Rockwell Corporation had various logos that included the letter "R." Some other logos you might

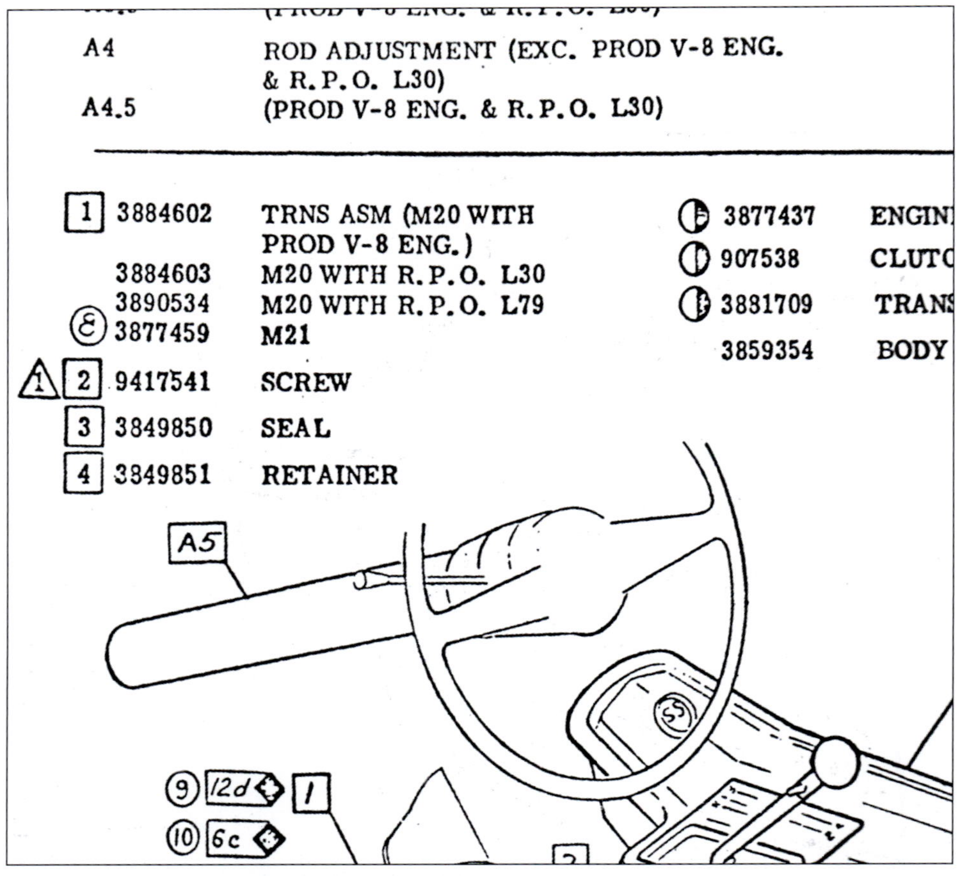


*This is a page from an old factory 1967 Nova assembly manual showing three different part numbers for the M20 and one number for the M21. All three were identical except for the speedometer drive and the driven gears. Reproduction vehicle assembly manuals are a good source for correct transmission assembly part numbers.*

come across are "KS," "RSC," and "D." Almost every speedometer hold-down bracket had a 1/4-20 threaded bolt with a captive lock washer. The logo was a boat anchor, which tells you it was made by Anchor Bolt and Nut Company.

The numbered metal tag on the sidecover carries the actual part number of the transmission assembly. Many part numbers exist for the same transmission because of different speedometer gear combinations across different model platforms. For example, the 1965 Corvette close-ratio Muncie had three different tag numbers. Most transmissions are missing these tags, but if you want to do a complete restoration they are generally necessary.

Even if your Muncie is assembled from a mix of parts, you should be able to determine the ratio. Remember, if the transmission is still in the car only the 1969 to 1974 cases had ratio identifiers in the serial number. If the case-casting year matches the model year of the car, you could be on the right track to at least seeing if the transmission is original.

*This is a good example of a bad restamp (or fake). Notice that the serial number has been ground off (left). P7 (1967 model year) was stamped on a 1968–1969 3925660 case.*

*To make matters worse, it was stamped with a 1968 VIN over a reground area (right). There is no point restamping a case unless you can do it right.*

# HOW MUNCIE 4-SPEEDS WORK

*The inner workings of a Muncie 4-speed can be intimidating at first. Once explained, you will see that it is quite easy to understand how every component functions.*

It is a good idea to understand the basics of your Muncie 4-speed before you start rebuilding the transmission. Successfully diagnosing transmission problems is directly related to how well you understand how this transmission works.

## Forward Gears

The Muncie 4-speed is a constant-mesh transmission. This means that all the gears in the transmission, except for reverse, are always meshed together and spinning, even in neutral. When you shift you are locking a particular-speed gear to the mainshaft. In reality, only three reduction gears correspond to physical first, second, and third gears. Fourth gear is technically a direct drive, so no physical gear is actually being used.

All forward-speed gears are locked to the output shaft via the two synchronizer assemblies; each assembly is responsible for working two gears. The rear assembly is the 1-2 and the front assembly is the 3-4. The cover has two shifter shafts that operate the forks, which then control the corresponding assemblies. The rear shaft works the 1-2 synchronizer fork; the forward shaft works the 3-4 synchronizer fork. The cover mechanism has detents that position and lock the shift fork in place. These detents function as interlocks, preventing any two forward-speed gears from being shifted at the same time. These also scissor in the sidecover.

Keep in mind that grabbing two gears at the same time can be extremely dangerous. In addition to blowing up the transmission, the driver can lose control of the car. When a shift is made, the shift fork moves the slider and the slider moves the three strut keys (or shift dogs). Finally, this energizes the synchro ring onto the gear. The synchro ring is locked to the synchro hub, which is then locked to the output shaft. Therefore, the ring matches the speed of the gear to the speed of the output shaft. (The ring is essentially a tapered cone clutch.) As the ring is forced against the cone of the gear the gear's speed is matched to the speed of the output shaft and the slider continues to lock the gear to the shaft. This action all happens in a split second.

## Reverse Gears

Reverse gear is a sliding gear. It has no ability to synchronize; therefore, you can only put a car into reverse when you are at a complete stop. The shifter shaft in the extension housing is the reverse shaft. The problem with this design is that it is very possible to shift into reverse and *one* of the forward-speed gears at the same time because no interlock mechanism is present. This doesn't happen often, but sometimes a bent shift rod may rub against another rod and you lock up the transmission.

Many people grind reverse because they are too impatient to wait for the transmission to slow down on its own. Sometimes people put the transmission into first gear to make sure the transmission has stopped turning before putting it into reverse. This is a pretty good practice providing you have proper clutch release to begin with.

Clutch release can also be checked using what I call a "reverse-gear spin-down test." Get your car good and warm so that all parts are hot and expanded while the engine is idling. With the transmission in neutral, press down on your clutch pedal, count off 10 seconds, and then put the transmission directly into reverse. This should be enough time for the transmission to slow down on its own so if there is any type of grind or clunk, the transmission is still turning when it should not, indicating poor release.

A clutch that releases poorly is the most common cause of synchro ring failure. In order for a synchronizer ring to do its job properly, it must be able to sync up the shaft and gear speeds with no engine load on it. If load is present, the ring overheats as it tries to fight the engine load; this causes the ring to warp.

The problem of falling out of gear is frequently misdiagnosed; people are very quick to blame synchro rings or shifter adjustment. Usually the cause is simply physical wear on the shift fork, the slider fork groove, the slider splines, and gear engagement teeth. Because the sidecover has positive detents these transmissions always shift into gear correctly with the shifter. The cover mechanism is very efficient in making sure that the shift fork moves the slider the correct amount. Basically, the cover is either in gear or its not; there is no adjustment. The only adjustment possible with this type of transmission is a linkage adjustment for a clean neutral gate.

## Lack of Front Seal

Unlike any other modern 4-speed, the Muncie has no front seal. The early T10 it replaced was also designed without a front seal. After 1965, the first-design Super T10 added a front seal, yet the Muncie never had one. Front oil leaks are a very common problem with these transmissions.

Without a front oil seal, oil must be directed away from the front bearing retainer input shaft opening. Oil is pushed away from this opening with an oil slinger and gland nut. The slinger is essentially a tin shield that blocks the opening and prevents oil from dumping through the front bearing from the inside. It still allows oil to lubricate the bearing but it keeps the majority of oil volume away from the bearing. While the slinger is spinning, it slings the oil away from the opening.

The gland nut is on the front side of the input; it is a left-hand-thread tapered nut that locks the front main bearing to the input shaft. When assembled, the tapered portion of the nut fits within .030 inch to a matching tapered portion of the front bearing retainer. This creates a "proximity seal." The left-hand thread of the input shaft protrudes into a cavity in the front retainer. As the transmission spins, these threads force oil back toward the inside of the transmission.

This operation was designed to work with non-synthetic 80- to 90-weight gear lube. The proximity seal requires this type of oil viscosity so it *cannot* easily flow around the nut and out of the front retainer. Using synthetic-based oils frequently causes leaks because they flow too easily and defeat the function of this system. Overfilling the transmission also causes leak issues since the oil fill plug is lower than the retainer opening. Because this system has no air vents, any air leak into the casing can cause leaks.

A bad rear seal that allows air into the system may also cause a front oil leak. Excessive driveshaft yoke movement due to excessive pinion angles or rear axle movement can turn the driveshaft yoke into a pump and cause oil to blow out of the front.

## Oil Specifications

*Muncie Oil Capacity: 1.25 to 1.50 Quarts of GL4/GL5 Manual Transmission Fluid*

The American Petroleum Institute (API) has a GL specification for gearbox lubricants. The API-GL specification number is an indication of the intended gear type, load, and material for the application. The numbering scale progresses upward for load-carrying ability. GL3 and GL4 products are primarily intended for low load automotive gearboxes and manual transmissions. Hypoid/GL5– and GL6-rated oils are intended for higher load applications such as differentials and rear axles.

A great deal of incorrect information is on the Internet regarding whether GL5-grade manual transmission fluids are harmful to synchro rings. I believe that there is some merit to this theory. However, in 33 years of servicing manual transmissions, I have never seen an issue where synchro rings failed due to corrosion from GL5 lubricant. Most synthetic oils, including Royal Purple's 75-90WT, meet GL4 and GL5 specifications. I have seen standard mineral-based oils from Castrol, Pennzoil, Torco, Valvoline, etc., with an 80- to 90-weight viscosity work well. If you are in extremely cold climates where shifting is difficult or intermittent grinding occurs until the transmission warms up you may want to consider a synthetic-based oil. The problem with some synthetic oils is that because the standard Muncie has no front seal, they tend to flow more easily and will leak out of the front.

## Design Features

The Muncie 4-speed was installed in a variety of high-performance GM cars throughout the 1960s and 1970s, including the Pontiac GTO, Chevelle, Camaro, Oldsmobile 442, Buick GS, and many others. The 4-speed functions the same, and its operation is fairly simple. All forward gears are independent of the mainshaft; the input gear engages the cluster gear; the splined synchro hub resides on the mainshaft; and the synchro ring engages the gear's cone so the slider can lock onto the gear's teeth.

*The bronze synchro ring has a 6-degree internal taper that matches the taper on the gear's synchro cone. As it is forced against the cone, it eventually causes the output shaft to run at the same speed as the gear. It's essentially what is called a cone clutch.*

*I have removed the hub so you can see how the strut key springs force the struts to track in the same direction the slider moves. These struts fit into a slot in the synchro ring. The struts apply pressure to the ring forcing it to energize against the spinning gear.*

*The detent combs are in the sidecover. The tips of the shift forks engage the slots in the comb. When you shift off the neutral position (N) the opposite end of the comb (X) stops the opposing side from moving. You can also see from the labeled first, second, third, and fourth positions that it really is impossible for a transmission to be partially in gear.*

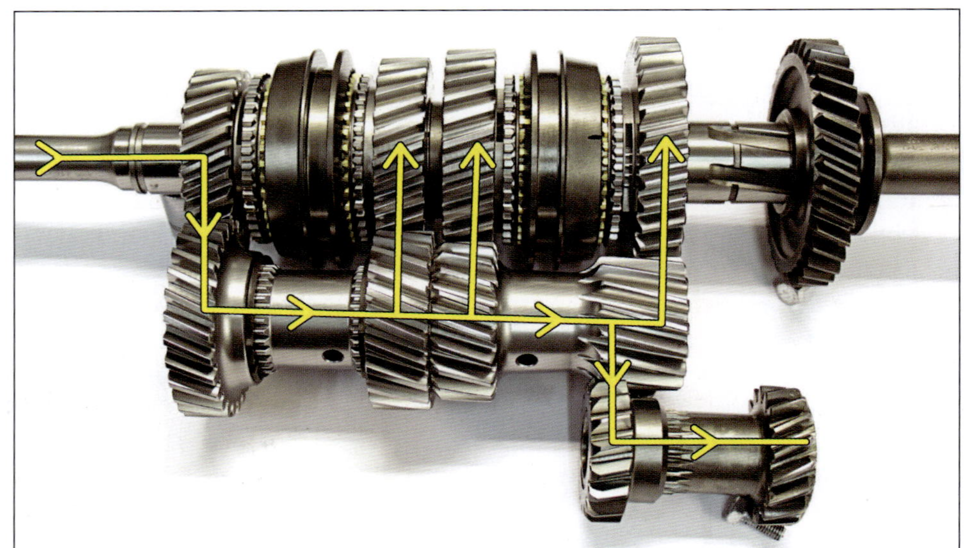

*This is the power flow of all gears in neutral. As you can see, all of the gears are in constant mesh. Power comes in from the input shaft and spins all the gears but nothing is transmitted to the output shaft.*

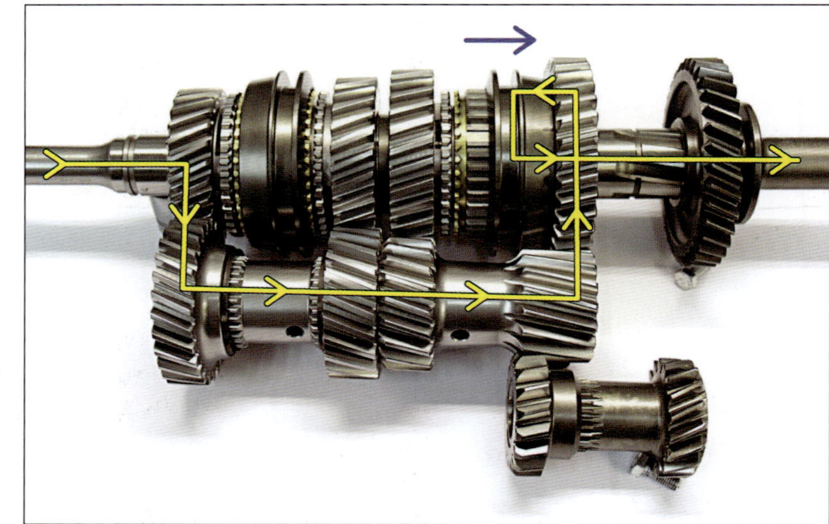

*First-gear power comes in from the input shaft, travels down into the countergear, and up through first gear. The slider is moved toward first gear, engaging it and locking it to the output shaft via the 1-2 synchronizer assembly. (The yellow line indicates the path and the blue arrow marks the direction of power flow.)*

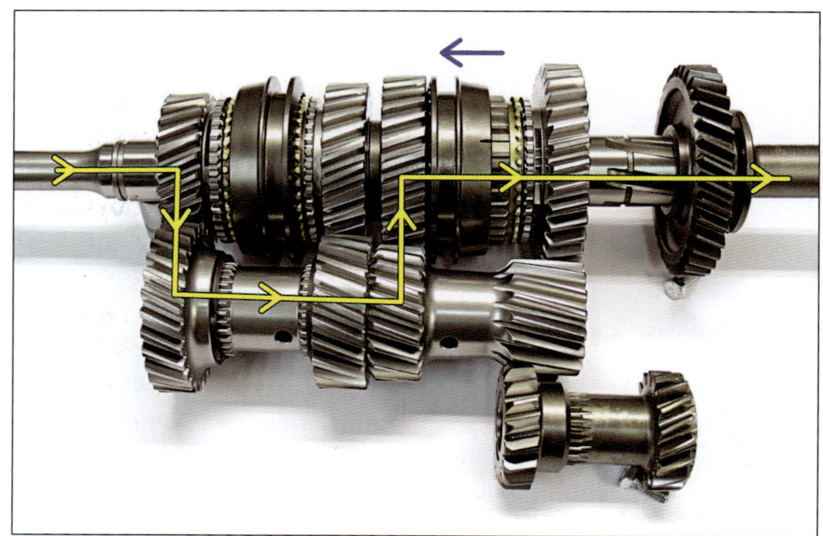

*Second-gear power comes in from the input shaft, travels down into the countergear, and up through second gear. The slider is moved toward second gear, engaging it and locking it to the output shaft via the 1-2 synchronizer assembly. (The yellow line indicates the path and the blue arrow marks the direction of movement.)*

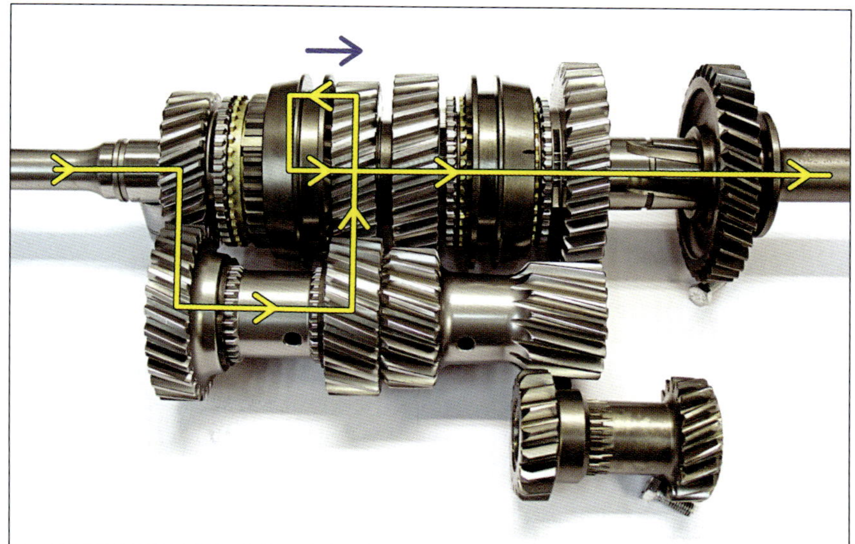

Third-gear power comes in from the input shaft, travels down into the countergear, and up through third gear. The slider is moved toward third gear, engaging it and locking it to the output shaft via the 3-4 synchronizer assembly. (The yellow line indicates the path and the blue arrow marks the direction of movement.)

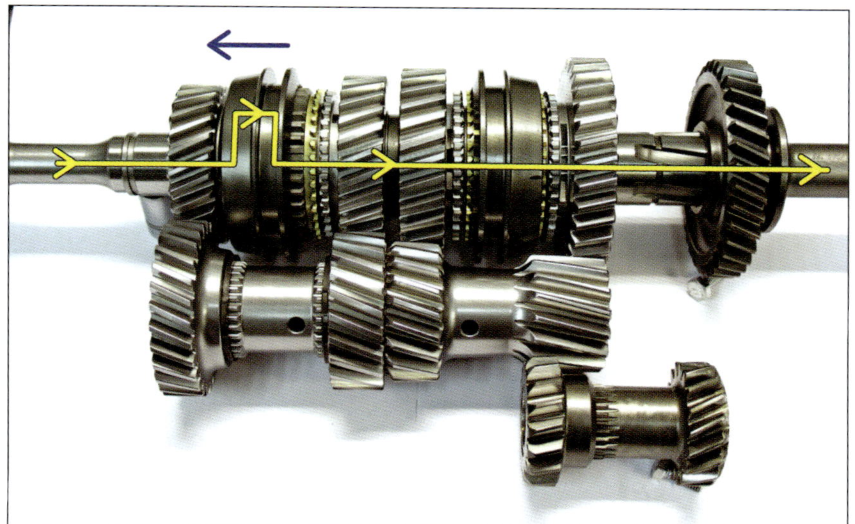

Fourth-gear power comes in from the input shaft and locks directly to the output shaft via the 3-4 synchronizer assembly. (The yellow line indicates the path and the blue arrow marks the direction of movement.) No gears are actually in use when in fourth or direct. The input and output shafts are essentially coupled together. All gears are freewheeling around the mainshaft.

Reverse-power comes in from the input shaft, travels down into the countergear, into the forward-reverse idler. The forward-reverse idler is coupled to a rear-reverse idler through a series of splines. This idler assembly rotates on the reverse-idler shaft. The reverse-mainshaft gear is moved forward to engage the idler. When gears are connected, the output shaft spins in the opposite rotation of the input shaft, and that gives you reverse. (The yellow line indicates the path, and the blue arrow marks the direction of movement.)

The input shaft has roller needle bearings that allow it to spin on the mainshaft. As the 3-4 slider locks it to the mainshaft, the rollers are no longer in motion. Transmissions with bad bearings often quiet down in fourth because the bearings have no load.

This image of an input shaft shows the position and direction of the gland nut. I've left the front bearing off so you can see its position. The factory stakes the nut into the hole in the threads with a punch. I just use red thread locker.

## Diagnosing Common Problems

Most rebuilds are initiated because a problem forces a repair. Some people just fix the problem and others choose to rebuild the transmission completely.

Let's say you have a front bearing problem. You have determined that the rumbling noise you hear is indeed the front bearing; you take the front bearing retainer cover off and your suspicions are confirmed.

Here the shaft and nut are in the front bearing retainer. The retainer has a machined taper that matches the nut. Just forward of the taper is a cavity into which the threads fit. When they're spinning, these left-hand threads act like an auger-style pump, pulling oil away from the opening. When it is still, the oil level is below this, and that's why you should never overfill a Muncie.

The tin oil slinger acts like a shield to block large volumes of oil from flowing through the front bearing. It also acts like a shim, moving the input shaft inward .030 inch. These should always be replaced during a rebuild.

You install a new bearing, replace the front gasket, clean up, reinstall the front retainer, and then reinstall the transmission, realign the shifter, and the noise is gone.

Judging from my volume of front bearing sales, this is a popular repair, but it is not a rebuild. You have to judge whether or not to make a repair or do a full rebuild. Sometimes you need to make a quick repair because time is a factor. It can also be an eco-

An anti-backlash plate was only put on the later M20 countergears. The teeth are offset with the main gear teeth. The plate is spring loaded with a circular spring and it floats on the three rivets. The concept is that in no-load conditions the gearset's backlash is eliminated to prevent the gears from chattering. I always remove these plates because the rivets tend to loosen and ruin the case and gears.

nomic question: A full rebuild with all new gears, shift forks, and sliders is simply out of the question. Several common shifting issues develop with most manual transmissions as well as Muncie 4-speeds. You need to correctly diagnose them so you can determine the best solution. However, diagnosing these issues can be difficult at times and extremely frustrating. Following are the problems Muncies tend to encounter.

### Gear and Bearing Noises

A whining noise that changes pitch with RPM is usually an indicator of worn gears and the common cause is lack of oil. If the maindrive section is worn it whines in all gears except fourth. If wear is present on first, second, or third gear, the noise is louder when loaded in that particular gear. Most low-oil issues affect the maindrive section because oil runs to the back of the transmission when moving forward, which starves the front end of lubrication and gouges out the centers of the gear teeth.

A knocking or banging noise that becomes faster or slower with RPM changes indicates one or several broken gear teeth. These noises don't go away when not under load because all the gears are in constant mesh. However, they may be louder when the broken gear is under load.

Rattle-type noises can be difficult to diagnose. Sometimes external vibration issues from tires or a driveshaft can cause parts in the transmission to rattle. I've seen linkage rods that rattle. Sliders that are loose on the hubs can cause rattles. Imperfections, dings, or high spots on gears can cause unloaded gears to rattle because the backlash becomes uneven. When under load, the rattle may actually quiet down. Worn shift forks that allow sliders to over-travel and bounce against the lower countergear or forward reverse idler are a common cause of whirring rattling noises.

Worn bearings don't whine or knock; they rumble. When bearings wear, the balls and raceways develop pits or craters. Because the raceways are rotating and the balls are spinning, the damaged portions of each component never contact each other in the exact same place. Therefore, bearing noise tends to sound like an erratic rumble.

A defective front bearing makes noise in neutral and all other gears. A bad rear bearing only makes noise when the driveshaft is turning or the car is in motion. Bearings make the most noise under load. In fourth gear, bearing noise tends to quiet down and sometimes goes away because the input and output shafts are locked together and there is no radial load on the bearings.

One design flaw in the Muncie that has proven to be an issue is front reverse idler gear chatter (mentioned above). Occasionally a transmission has an erratic chattering noise only in first gear. Inspect the forward side of the front idler. Usually the 1-2 slider rubs against the idler when in first-gear position. This happens when the shift fork or slider's groove wears, which allows it to travel rearward too much and it fouls against the idler. Almost all disassembled Muncies show signs of this problem.

### Grinding

A shift that produces a scrape or a grind means that the bronze synchronizer ring is not working properly. Rings wear and eventually go bad. Ring life can be prolonged by keeping the oil clean, which reduces abrasion wear, and also by making sure you have correct clutch release.

Poor clutch release is the number-one killer of synchro rings. Rings have to work harder if the clutch release is not clean; they tend to get hot and warp. In addition, shifting without a clutch promotes ring wear, as does harsh power shifting (and we all love to power shift our Muncies!). The definition of power shifting is to keep your accelerator pedal mashed to the floor as you shift through all four gears. Rings tend to bend and warp from this type of abuse and that's why more expensive "harder" forged rings are necessary for this application. If the ring is no longer concentric with the gear's synchro cone it does not lock onto the gear efficiently.

### Hard Shifting and Grinding in Reverse

It's amazing that many people don't understand the function of the clutch. The clutch simply disengages the transmission from the engine so you can shift it. When you shift the transmission with no engine load on it, the synchros are allowed to properly work and couple the selected gear to the output shaft. Even though your clutch may be new, it still may not be releasing properly.

Reverse is a non-synchro gear, so the transmission must be stopped to engage it properly. If it grinds, that means it's still turning and thus still connected to the engine. The clutch fork pivot ball and release bearing length all play an important part in aiding in a good release. The old notion of adjusting a clutch for a certain amount of free play does not work if your clutch fork pivot angle is off because the pivot places it too far away from the clutch cover. You need to mock up everything, especially when purchasing special clutches where finger heights and flywheel heights vary from the factory specs.

### Jumping Out of Gear

Because Muncie gear teeth are machined with a helical angle to them they thrust forward or backward depending on whether you are accelerating or decelerating. Proper clearances need to be maintained to keep individual-speed gears connected to the sliders as they transmit power to the output shaft. The shift forks that control the sliders are stationary. In a sense, they are attached to the main case via the sidecover. If the geartrain is allowed to move forward or backward you can have a fall-out issue.

The rear bearing locates the whole geartrain in the center midplate of the transmission. I have often seen the aluminum midplate retainer develop severe wear in the locating snap-ring groove. This allows movement of the whole mainshaft assembly.

Jumping out of gear has nothing to do with the synchro rings themselves. It is physical wear on any or all of the clutch's gear teeth or slider teeth. It can also be that the slider shift fork groove is too wide.

All speed gears have 36 clutch teeth each. When they are new they have a nice point. If a synchro ring fails and the transmission (when shifted) grinds into a particular gear, these teeth wear. The matching splined teeth on the slider also wear. If enough material wears away on the gear and the matching slider, the transmission may produce harsh shifting or just not stay in gear.

When I inspect gears and sliders I look for good point definition on both pieces. If the teeth are blunt or worn more than half their original length, both gear and slider are replaced. If I am using used gears with some clutch tooth wear I usually use a new torque-locking slider. These sliders have a back taper to their internal spline. The spline is machined and is narrowed toward the center of the slider. Under load, whether you are on or off the throttle, the clutch tooth of the gear is forced to follow down the taper of the spline toward the center of the slider and stay in gear.

Shift forks usually show obvious signs of wear. The thickness of new forks measures approximately .360 to .365 inch. The problem with fork wear is that the forks never wear evenly. If the fork pad is not flat and is tapered, it accelerates wear on the slider groove.

### Block-Out Conditions

Sometimes the transmission just does not shift. You have checked the clutch, it is releasing correctly, and you are not getting a grind. Remember, if you are attempting to shift and you get a grind, the synchro ring is *not* doing its job. It cannot grab the gear and slow it down to match the speed of the output shaft.

So what happens when you try to make a shift and it feels like you hit a dead stop? This is called "blocking out," an indexing issue that is the result of one of two different scenarios.

One, the synchro ring, when energized, is allowed to over-travel in relation to the hub. This allows the slider to hit the ring point-to-point and block it from going over the ring. Worn strut key slots in the ring, worn strut keys, or the hub's key slots can cause it.

Two, the slider itself could be at fault. The points of the slider teeth often become so flat or skewed to one side that they prevent the slider from going over the ring.

### Leaks and Vibrations

As Muncie 4-speeds age, physical wear takes it toll on case components such as seals and shafts. As a result, leaks and vibrations often develop. Sidecover shifter shaft bores can elongate over time because the design has a steel shaft running in an aluminum housing. Vibrations are usually related to tires, driveshaft, and piloting issues. To help with diagnosis, make a note if certain leaks only happen while driving, or a vibration occurs all the time or in a specific gear (for example).

Factory Muncies have no front seal and used a slinger system. Overfilling causes leaks. Bad sidecover and rear-seal leaks are quite common. Another common issue is a leak coming from the front countergear bore as its press fit wears and becomes elongated.

Use of synthetic oils causes leaks in Muncies. The front nut oil slinger system was designed to work with conventional 80- or 90-weight oils. Synthetic oil flows much better and tends to work its way past the front gland nut. I've noticed that cars with bad trailing arm or leaf spring bushings can promote front oil leaks. If the driveshaft is moving so that the front yoke reciprocates in and out of the rear housing, it acts like a pump and blows oil out the front of the transmission. Never install an air vent in a Muncie unless you have a front seal. Letting air into the system allows oil to dump out of the unsealed front portion faster.

For the Muncie to function properly it has to be accurately piloted on both the input and output shafts. All Muncie inputs outside the car move up and down. Therefore, if you wiggle the input shaft you will see that the output moves as well. If you apply downward pressure to the output shaft you are not able to move the input. These transmissions rarely vibrate. You can have noisy main bearings but if the transmission is piloted correctly it does not vibrate. New extension housing bushings and driveshaft yokes usually have no more than .005-inch clearance. That's only .0025 on the surface. If the yoke, rear bushing, or pilot bushing is worn, you can get a vibration. It's rarely a mainshaft or input shaft, because if the shafts were bent to a point that would cause a vibration, the extension housing would break because of the tight bushing clearance.

### Clutch Issues

Problems with the clutch can easily affect how your transmission shifts and feels. Clutch and flywheel imbalances can frequently cause vibrations that migrate into the gearbox. A clutch that has a poor release

# Clutch or Transmission Problem?

**S**ometimes the transmission can have issues that masquerade as clutch problems and vice versa. The following photos illustrate some things to watch for. All photos are courtesy of Centerforce Performance Clutch. ■

*The clutch disc is connected to the input shaft spline so the transmission pilots its hub. The bellhousing must be concentric on the engine's crankshaft centerline. If the bellhousing is not concentric with the engine's crankshaft centerline, the splines wear prematurely and the hub fractures.*

*Hot spots indicate that the clutch has been slipping, which usually shows on the flywheel and pressure plate. Clutch chattering and slipping are a common symptom. Sometimes the clutch is not fully released or the disc has contamination from engine or transmission oil leaks. Your driving style can also be the culprit.*

*Bent or broken drive straps can cause difficult clutch engagement, hard shifting, and clutch rattles. Severe/abusive downshifting, missed shifts, or harsh use of engine braking typically cause this damage.*

## Clutch or Transmission Problem? *CONTINUED*

The counterweights' backside was hitting the clutch disc. This is what happens when you have too much travel. Over-centering the diaphragm spring or clutch fingers (arrows) pushes the disc against the flywheel, which causes a release and noise problem.

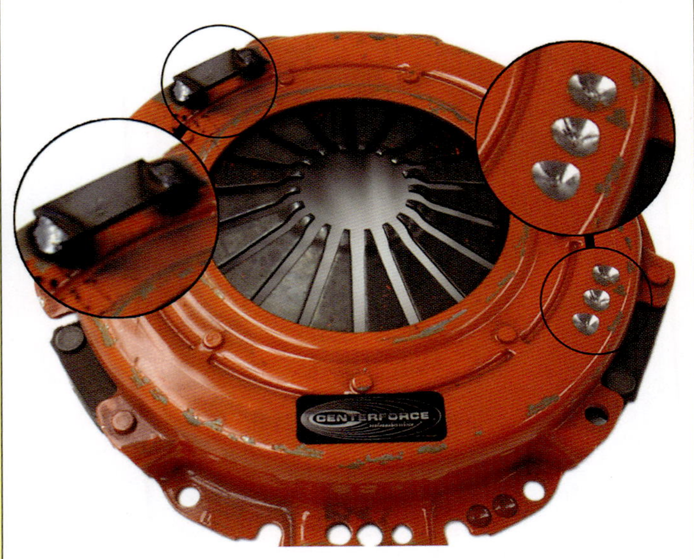

This welded and drilled clutch cover shows the results of a poorly executed balance job. Sometimes these clutch covers haven't been properly balanced and vibrations tend to migrate to the engine and transmission. People frequently try to add weight to the clutch cover because they have the wrong counterweighted flywheel.

An engine or transmission oil leak has contaminated this disc. This accelerates clutch disc wear, and consequently causes slipping and chattering.

Bent clutch covers such as this are rare, but this condition causes shifting issues and clutch chatters. Dropping a cover, using the wrong hardware, or bolting down the cover with debris under it causes this damage.

The clutch you fit to your engine must be rated to handle the torque load. If your clutch cannot handle the load, it may end up looking like this: an overloaded disc ready to come apart. In addition to slippage, chatters, and vibrations, you will probably smell it.

Springs drive the clutch hub and the stop rivets limit the hub's motion. If you sidestep the clutch at high RPM or rapidly jump on and off the throttle, the stop rivets take a beating, and then clutch noises and knocks are often heard when shifting. In addition, the hub springs may become fatigued from overheating and allow this to happen.

Clutch engagement and disengagement issues occur if you are missing chunks of your disc's lining. Abusive upshifts, downshifts, and missed shifts can cause this. Discs that are bonded and riveted are less likely to have this issue.

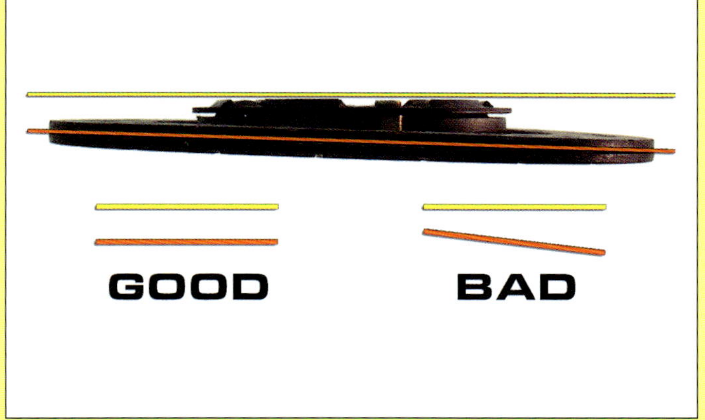


The proper air gap is important to ensure a good clutch release. If your disc is bent, you have release issues that, of course, create shifting issues. This disc was bent because a transmission was allowed to hang from it during an install. Always check new discs for flatness because they can become damaged in shipping.

# Clutch or Transmission Problem? *CONTINUED*

In most cases, flywheel bolts have special heads on them. It's still a standard hex head but usually it's shallow compared to a typical bolt of the same thread size. Because of the variety of companies offering products these days, we find ourselves mixing components from different manufacturers. It's important that you take the time to put the flywheel side of the disc against the flywheel surface and check for clearance issues before bolting up the clutch assembly. The hub's springs may have been the wrong size or the bolts used may have been too big, causing the wear seen in this picture.

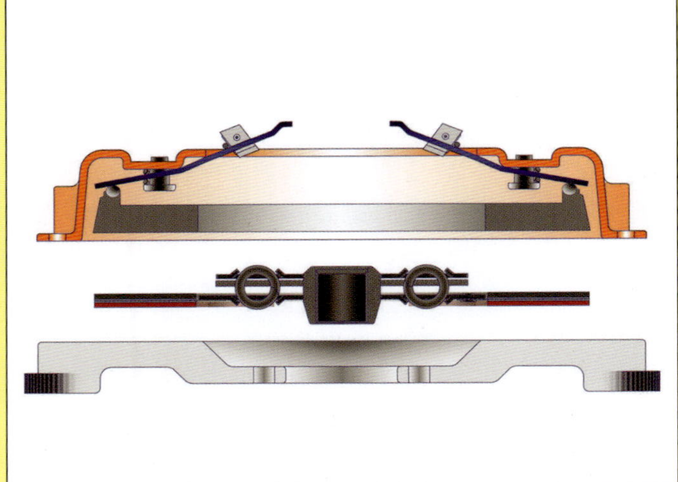

This is a cross section of a typical single-disc system. When the clutch lining is clamped between the engine's flywheel and clutch pressure plate, the dampening springs drive the clutch hub, which is splined to the transmission's input shaft. The input shaft transmits power through the transmission and to the rear axle. If your flywheel is too light, you can get low- or no-load gearbox rattles because the hub's springs are not staying evenly loaded through each firing cycle. These harmonic vibrations increase when using light flywheels with 6- or 4-cylinder applications.

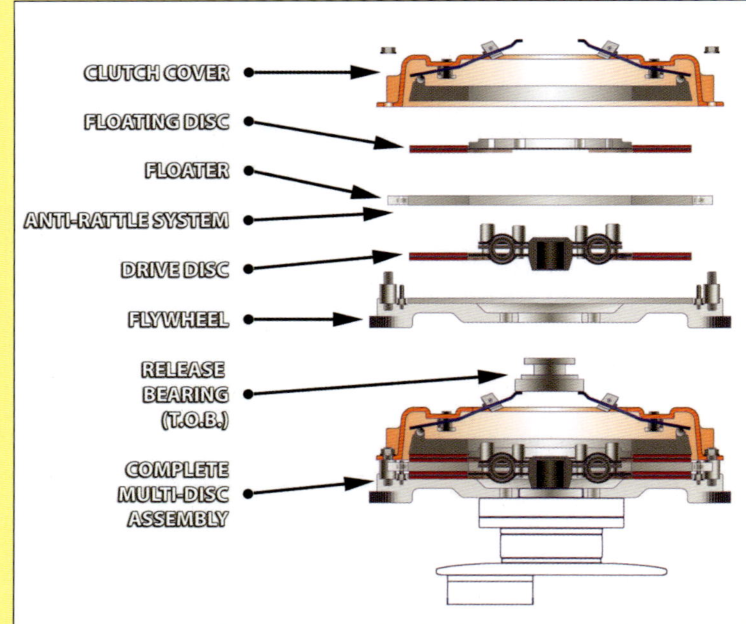


This is a Centerforce DYAD multi-clutch system. This compact dual-disc system allows two discs to be used in the same space as a single-disc system.

*You must check* everything, *and that includes all new parts. I often have seen bearings placed on the adapter housings backward. It only takes a little effort to do these simple checks and balances but it will save you time in the long run. (Photo Courtesy Centerforce Performance Clutch)*

causes hard shifting and premature synchro ring failure. The front bearing retainer of a Muncie is made of soft cast iron. The clutch release bearing or throwout bearing can, over time, chew up the retainer and create a "notchy" feel to your clutch pedal.

Replacement clutch release bearings and clutch forks tend to vary in size. It is important that you take the time to mock up the fork and release bearing to make sure you have the correct free play as well as enough throw. Two types of release bearings are generally used: flat face and round face. The flat-face bearing is used with any pressure plate that has fingers that protrude out of the cover at an angle. The round face is used when the fingers are flat within the cover. A round-face bearing allows the fingers to roll over the bearing.

## Shifter Considerations

When faced with a shifting issue it is often difficult to distinguish between problems that are shifter related and those that are transmission related. Learning how a shifter works should clear up some common misconceptions.

### Shifter Shafts

First, you need to understand what the shifter can and cannot do. Muncie transmissions have three shifter shafts. All forward gears are in the sidecover, which has a detent and interlock system.

The shifter shaft is in the tail and works independently. The throw of the shifter is limited by the detents in the Muncie sidecover. The shifter does not control throw, but does control how it feels. The terms "long-throw" or "short-throw" shifter relate to how much movement the shifter's stick has from its neutral position to a specific gear. The stick itself moves in an arc. The shifter's design as well as its linkage shift arms affect the geometry of the arc and how the shifter is controlled. The shorter the arc, the shorter the throw, but the higher the shift effort. Conversely, the longer the arc, the longer the throw, and the lower the shift effort. Basically, what you have is a lever. The more leverage you have, the easier the shift effort is.

Sometimes shifter throw can be too long, especially for performance use. If the throw is longer, more time is spent shifting from one gear to another. Companies such as Hurst and Long design short-throw shifters. Some shift effort is sacrificed for a more positive, shorter throw.

The Hurst Competition/Plus shifter was designed in the early 1960s, and patented on November 9, 1965. Because it came out when the Muncie became popular, it was offered as a dealer add-on option. It was offered in the Pontiac GTO as the standard shifter for the Muncie starting in 1964 and was also the standard shifter in the Olds 442 and Chevy Camaro.

### Neutral Adjustment

Regardless of the shifter you are using, the shifter body incorporates three gates: the 1-2 gate, the 3-4 gate, and the reverse gate. The gate connects your stick to the specific linkage arm you are using and is connected by a linkage rod. For example, the 1-2 gate connects to the 1-2 shift arm using the 1-2 rod.

The *only* adjustment you can make in any of these floor shifters is a *neutral* adjustment. With a neutral adjustment you are matching the neutral position of the transmission's shifter shafts with the neutral position of the shifter's gates. Whether you install a factory Muncie shifter or Hurst shifter, it's all the same. You can possibly make a minor adjustment to the shifter stop bolts on aftermarket shifters that have them.

When you make a shift, you only are moving the shifter either forward or backward. A stop bolt is located in either side of the shifter's body so that the shifter mechanism, when fully in gear, bumps against the stop bolt.

To adjust stops, first unscrew them out of the shifter body. Next, place the shifter in a forward gear and turn the forward stop in until it contacts the internal mechanism's body. Repeat the same adjustment for the backward motion.

Stops absorb the shock load of the sidecover's detent combs. When you power shift a Muncie, the force of the shift is against the stop and it is not trying to over-shift the internal mechanism, which would possibly cause damage to it. If your stops are adjusted too far they may prevent the transmission from going fully into gear.

## Hurst Linkage Tips and Disassembly

Here are a few tips I've learned over the years regarding Hurst shifter disassembly, repair, and installation.

The left linkage arm is from a factory Muncie shifter. Note how the linkage arms and rods are positioned. the lower position gives a shorter throw than the upper. Hurst makes the arm on the right. The rod hole is placed between the GM holes.

This is the correct placement of the linkage arms in neutral. They should always face up; in reverse they should always face down. Hurst arms should never be canted forward in neutral; they are either straight or canted toward the back. Take note that the arms are bent and the position of the rods. This is typical of most Hurst shifters for Muncies.

If your linkage arms are facing downward, the "H" pattern of the shifter is reversed. This is a common misdiagnosis; people think something is backward in the gearbox.

Cleaning up a Hurst shifter helps your Muncie shift smoother and more easily. Most shifters had a tin dust shield that always got lost. Grit sticks to the grease and becomes embedded in the mechanism, which promotes wear. You can find these shields online from people selling Hurst parts. You can get all the internals to rebuild your shifter, so take the time to disassemble, clean, and inspect it.

## 1 Extract Main Pivot Pin

*Squirt some penetrating oil into the shifter to loosen the main pivot pin. You may have to tap the case with a hammer to get it to move. Once it's loose, pull it out with pliers.*

## 2 Remove Rear Plate

*I use two punches to spread the back end of the case open to remove the rear plate. Once you dislodge it, it pops right out.*

## 3 Remove Nut, Plate and Washer

*Remove the stick pivot nut, the hold-down plate, and the nylon washer.*

*Professional Mechanic Tip*

## 4 Pull Parts from Main Body

*You can grab all the internals and pull everything out of the main body in one shot. The steel spring shim plates can be very sharp so be sure to use caution and wear protective gloves. This area of the internal components can be tricky. It can be very helpful to take a photo of the components' positions.*

## 5 Clean and Organize All Parts

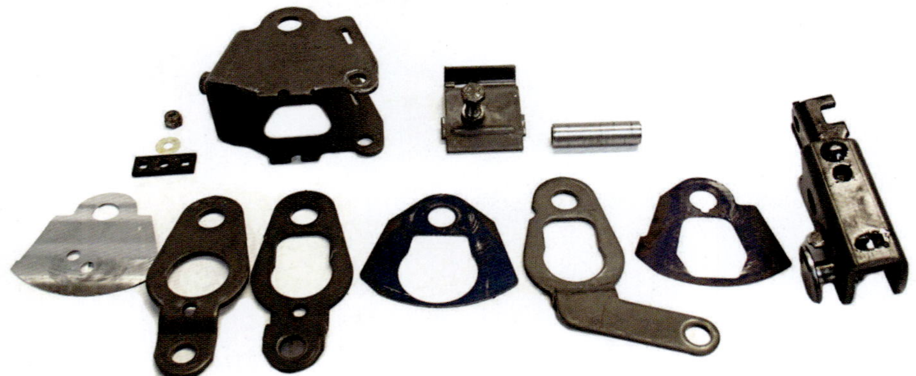

I've cleaned all the parts and laid them out so you can see how simply the shifter is made. A few shim plates, three shims, and a pivot mechanism for the stick is really all that makes it work.

## 6 Inspect Pivot Pin, Spring and Plunger

The stick pivots on the bolt and moves the plunger (bottom). The upper spring biases the plunger in the 3-4 gate and the lower spring gives the extra needed effort to get it into reverse. Try to avoid taking this apart unless you have to replace the plunger. I have often seen the lower pins bend; I replaced them with spiral-rolled pins instead of split pins.

## 7 Inspect for Plunger Wear

You can see how the plunger engages the 3-4 gate. Shifter slop is due primarily to worn rod bushings. However, I have seen plunger wear and the elongated gates that cause excess shifter movement.

## 8 Stack and Insert Parts in Housing

Once you have finished the inspection and cleaning, simply stack the parts on top of one another, slide them back into the body, and reverse the disassembly steps.

## 9 Back Out Stops

These are the stops. When reinstalling a shifter, always back them out and make a fresh adjustment. This is a standard 3/8-24 bolt. If the threads are worn out they are easy to source and replace.

## 10 Inspect Mount Plate

*Hurst makes shifters for their intended use. This mount plate can work on both the 27- and 32-spline Muncie extension housings. This plate is useful if you are putting a 1970 Camaro shifter in a 1972 Chevelle, for example. Rods and installation kits are model specific, but sometimes you can change a few items to make it all fit.*

## 11 Align Gates

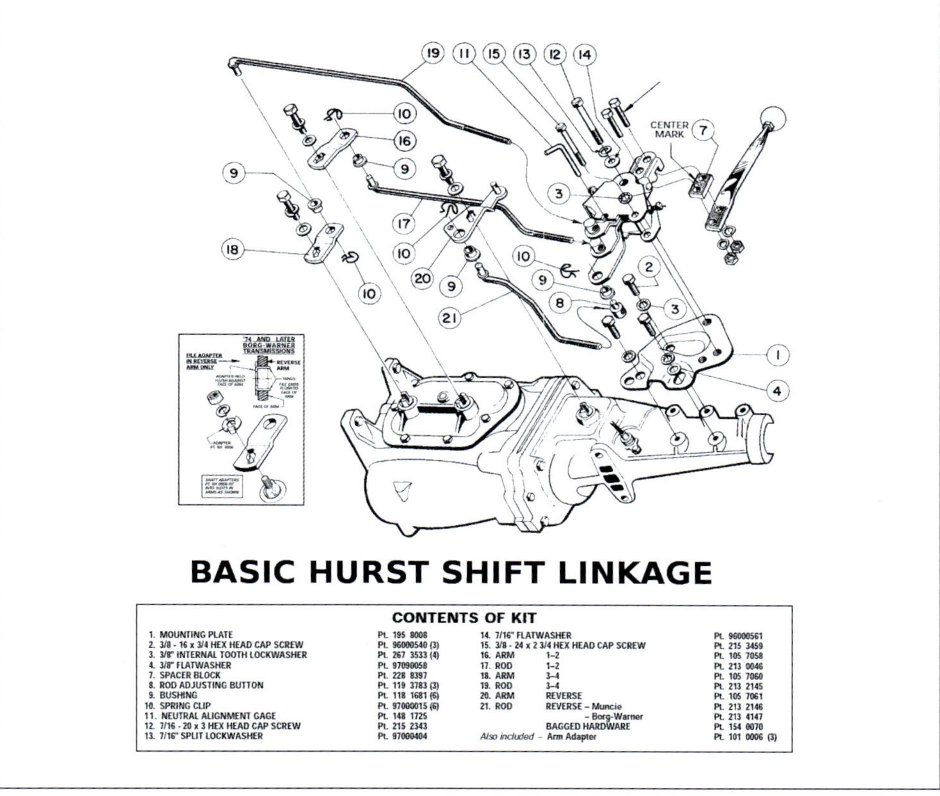

*If you don't have the Hurst alignment tool, you can always use a 1/4-inch drill bit to align the gates within the shifter's body to make your neutral adjustment.*

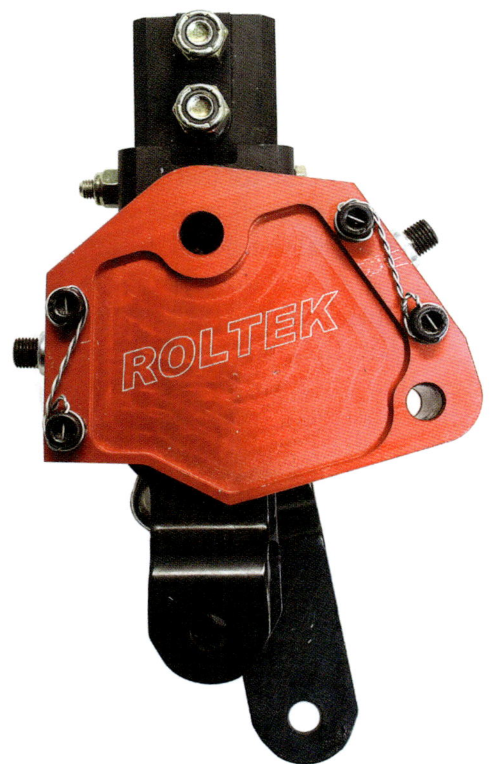

*Roltek offers an aluminum billet shifter that works on a standard Hurst mount. This shifter replaces the old Hurst Super Speedway shifter and uses a push-down lockout for reverse.*

**BASIC HURST SHIFT LINKAGE**

| | CONTENTS OF KIT | | |
|---|---|---|---|
| 1. MOUNTING PLATE | Pt. 195 8008 | 14. 7/16" FLATWASHER | Pt. 96000561 |
| 2. 3/8 - 16 x 3/4 HEX HEAD CAP SCREW | Pt. 96000540 (3) | 15. 3/8 - 24 x 2 3/4 HEX HEAD CAP SCREW | Pt. 215 3459 |
| 3. 3/8" INTERNAL TOOTH LOCKWASHER | Pt. 267 3533 (4) | 16. ARM 1–2 | Pt. 105 7058 |
| 4. 3/8" FLATWASHER | Pt. 97090058 | 17. ROD 1–2 | Pt. 213 0046 |
| 7. SPACER BLOCK | Pt. 228 8397 | 18. ARM 3–4 | Pt. 105 7060 |
| 8. ROD ADJUSTING BUTTON | Pt. 119 3783 (3) | 19. ROD 3–4 | Pt. 213 2145 |
| 9. BUSHING | Pt. 118 1681 (6) | 20. ARM REVERSE | Pt. 105 7061 |
| 10. SPRING CLIP | Pt. 97000015 (6) | 21. ROD REVERSE – Muncie | Pt. 213 2146 |
| 11. NEUTRAL ALIGNMENT GAGE | Pt. 148 1725 | – Borg-Warner | Pt. 213 4147 |
| 12. 7/16 - 20 x 3 HEX HEAD CAP SCREW | Pt. 215 2343 | BAGGED HARDWARE | Pt. 154 0070 |
| 13. 7/16" SPLIT LOCKWASHER | Pt. 97000404 | *Also included* – Arm Adapter | Pt. 101 0006 (3) |

*This is a typical exploded view of a Hurst Competition Plus shifter. All parts have numbers stamped on them to help you with placement of the rods and arms. This is how a Hurst Competition Plus shifter typically installs on a Muncie 4-speed. Both sidecover shift arms face up and the reverse arm faces down. Notice that the 1-2 arm bends toward the cover and the 3-4 arm bends away from the cover. The 1-2 rod goes behind its arm and the 3-4 rod is in front of its arm. The reverse rod also attaches on the outside of its arm. (Photo Courtesy of Hurst Shifters)*

---

# INSPECTION AND REPAIR

*I like using steak knives to remove gaskets. Never use an abrasive wheel or a sanding disc attached to an orbital grinder. You don't want to change the surface height by adding more valleys to it with a sander. Use a knife, some steel wool, or a wire wheel. You can use a file to true the gasket surface, making sure it is flat when all the gasket material is removed.*

Everyone has a different approach to prioritizing inspection, repair, and assembly. I like to start with the case components first and then deal with the internals second, during inspection. If you are doing this for the first time, remember that there is a huge difference between a restoration and a plain rebuild.

The difference is that with a restoration you restore all components as well as possible to their original specifications and look, which takes time, patience, and attention to many different details. Mechanically, the transmission should perform the same as when new.

If you are going to use paint use correct colors unless it is a street rod and it has a color theme. You can purchase cast iron– and aluminum-colored paint. I just don't like paint. I've seen too many transmissions come in with layers of paint over dirt; sometimes paint can hide cracks.

## Cleaning

It is generally not worth investing in a cleaning tank for just one job. You can usually take all of your components to a local transmission shop and pay them to run your parts through one of their industrial-size washers.

Small hobbyist cleaning tanks are fairly cheap from places such as Northern Hydraulics and Harbor Freight. You can use a paintbrush and odorless mineral spirits as a cleaning solution. Wear Nitrile gloves to protect your hands. Latex gloves come apart with mineral spirits. Always wear safety glasses.

## External Case Components

The main case, extension housing, sidecover, midplate, and front bearing retainer are all external case components. You must visually inspect for cracks, stripped bolt-hole threads, spun extension housing bushings, and previous repairs such as welds. Poorly welded cases can end up warping. I've seen gear

*It's quite common to see people dimple the front with a punch to stretch the metal back. I have also seen examples where people have aggressively chiseled a circular valley around the bore (thus closing the hole) and welded over the chiseled surface. The problem with these repairs is that they do not restore the case to its original centers. They just patch the leak.*

*The front countershaft bore often leaks oil when the case has been stressed. Usually the shaft falls out of the front because the surrounding metal has been pushed away from the shaft.*

centerlines go out of parallel because the case was not properly fixtured and overheated during welding.

Nowdays, most case components have damaged threads. The worse thing you can do is to drill and tap it to the next thread size rather than repair the thread properly.

### Main Case

Common issues are cracked, broken, or welded mounting ears and elongated countershaft holes. Front bearings can explode, spin, and damage the front bearing bore. Original cases had a magnet epoxied to the bottom of the case. The problem with that idea is that they eventually come loose. A loose magnet around metal gears causes some serious damage. You should remove the magnet and invest in magnetic fill and drain plugs.

*Steve Bechtold installed new bushings in the front and back of the case that's used for this book's rebuild; this procedure also restores the centers. He has a special fixture for machining and bushing the case. When it's completed, it will have a tight shaft press fit and no more leaks. The bore is honed to fit the countershaft I am using. Notice that he also added four new threaded inserts to the front bearing retainer's bolt threads.*

*Some people only repair the front bore to correct leakage issues. You need to repair both front and back bores if you want to make sure upper and lower shaft centers are properly spaced and back in parallel.*

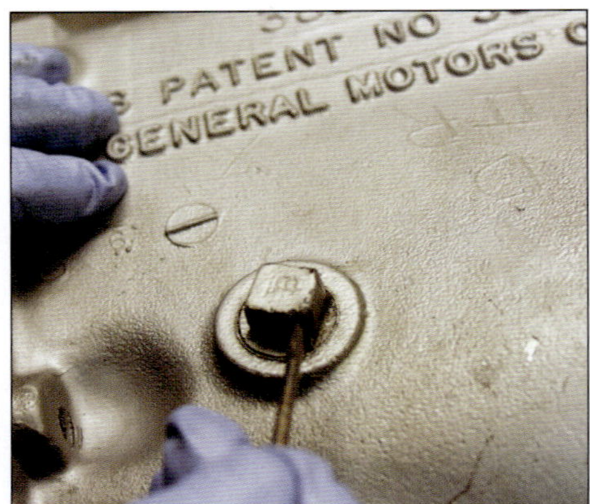

*The fill plug was over-torqued and the plug was also damaged. Most cases do not come with a drain plug. The fill thread must be repaired.*

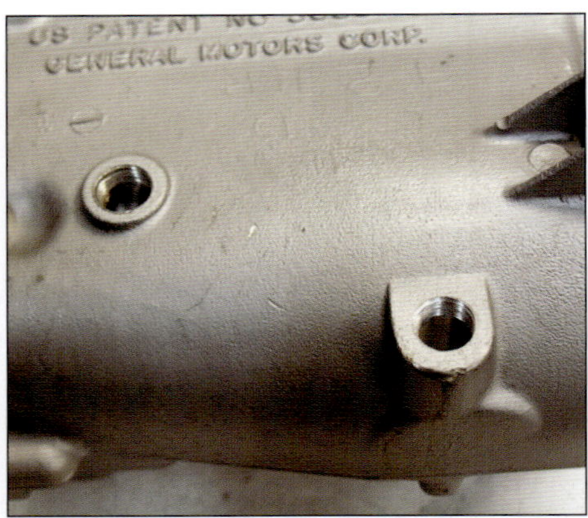

*A drain-plug hole and thread were added. The hole was drilled in steps from 3/8 to a 23/32-inch hole then threaded with a 1/2-inch NPT pipe tap.*

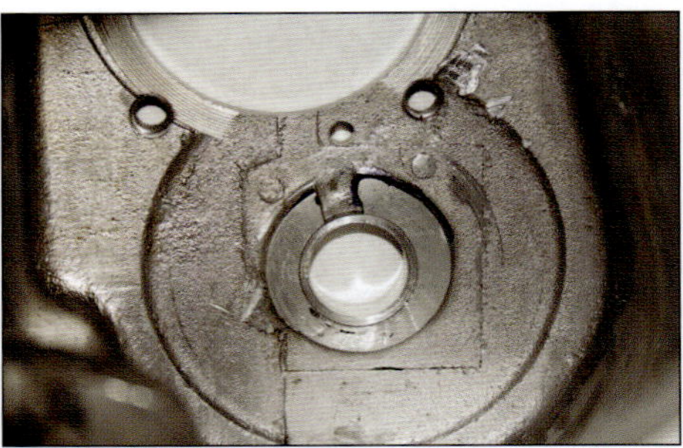

*Thrust washer surfaces inside the case are often damaged from spinning. This case had both surfaces welded and milled flat. This also gives a more positive surface for the washer's tang to lock against.*

Elongated front countershaft holes are the number-one cause of front case oil leaks. They can be repaired by boring the hole oversize and sleeving it with a bushing.

### Tailhousing

Stripped threads are common on the main case as well as on both the shifter and transmission mount pad. The reverse shifter shaft boss is damaged on most from people trying to remove a seized tapered lock pin. Spun bushings are rare, but if your bushing has fallen out (from spinning and damaging its bore), you need a new extension.

## Paint Removal

### 1 Strip Paint from Case

*I don't like paint. If you don't either, you can get metal serving trays from the Dollar Store and heavily brush the case components with paint stripper. I like using the paste type from RediStrip.*

### 2 Clean Case

*You can see how nice the finish of the aluminum is under the paint. If your case has some corrosion or bad discoloration showing after it has been washed off, you might put it in a glass-bead-blasting cabinet to add a more uniform finish to it.*

## 3 Repair Damaged Threads

Fix-A-Thred systems are available from most auto parts stores to repair damaged threads. You drill the damaged threaded hole to a specific size to accept a special tap.

## 4 Repair Damaged Threads
### CONTINUED

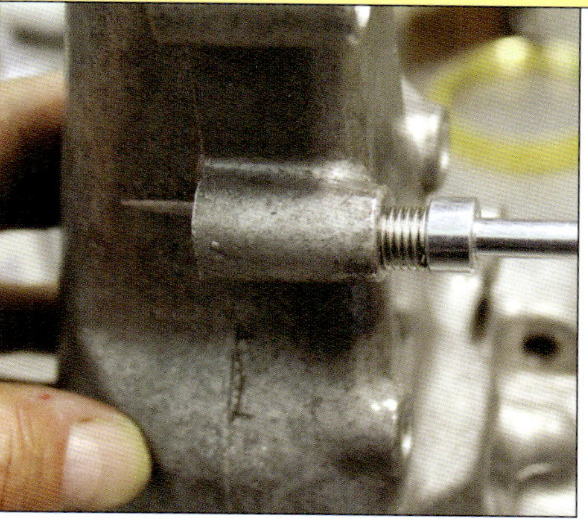

Screw a threaded insert into the new threaded hole that you just tapped. It maintains the old size internally.

## 5 Repair Damaged Threads
### CONTINUED

Once the insert has been installed, break off the drive tang. If the other mount threads are fine, just chase them with a 3/8-16 bottom tap and then chamfer the holes to center the incoming bolt.

## 6 Remove Damaged Reverse Pin

Sometimes people try to smash out a seized reverse-tapered pin. As a result, the pin's end is spread, which makes it impossible to drive the pin out. You have to grind out a portion of the lower end to free up the pin.

## 7 Remove Damaged Reverse Pin
### CONTINUED

Here, someone tried to drill out the pin from the bottom but missed the pin and then bent it within the bore. If this happens to you, you can use a hacksaw and slice down until you can lift the pin out. You still have a portion of the pinhole to work with after you weld it up.

## 8 Drill and Ream Pin Bore

Once you've built it all up with enough weld material, use a 1/8-inch drill bit to make a clean hole and then follow up with a No. 0 tapered reamer. Check the pin fit and ream until you like the fit. Once the pin fit is corrected, use a reamer in the shifter shaft bore to clean it up.

*Sidecover*

Sidecovers often leak, not because the seals wear out, but because the shifter shaft bores become elongated. Covers are not rare, so if a cover is cracked or the shift shafts wobble in the bores, just get another cover.

## Prep for Sidecover Disassembly

### 1 Inspect Sidecover

*This cover appears to have cracks, but these are just typical casting flaws that are not porous and are of no concern.*

### 2 Replace Pin

*The pin that holds the detent cams on this cover has no hat so it can fall in. Always replace these with a hat-style pin.*

### 3 Inspect Combs

*Inspect the detent comb for wear. This level of wear can cause a falling out of gear issue and a sloppy shift-feel.*

*You also need to be sure that the combs are straight. Laying them on a flat surface shows clearly if they are bent. You can see that these combs are bent. Bent combs bind against each other.*

### 4 Straighten Combs

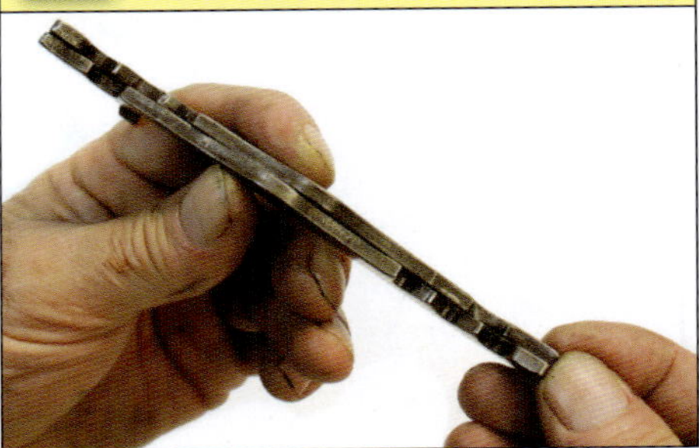

*To straighten the combs, place them in a vise. Gently tap them in place with a hammer so they sit against each other. Deburr the edges of the combs. They should be able to pass over each other smoothly.*

*Critical Inspection*

### 5 Inspect Shift Forks

*Inspect all shift forks for surface and detent tip wear. This fork has a broken tip and some pad wear. New fork pads are .360 to .362 inch thick. If yours are less than .350 inch, it's best to replace the fork to restore a positive shift feel.*

### 6 Inspect Linkage Arm

*If a linkage arm gets loose, it damages the rectangular key of the shifter shaft. This is a small 5/16-inch coarse-thread shaft, which is prone to breaking. Shift linkage arms must sit on the shaft tightly; if not, they always loosen. As a rule, the arm cannot move at all when it's attached to the shaft. This shaft is garbage.*

*If the front bearing nut is installed backward or it just loosens up, it rubs against the inside surface and leaks oil. New retainers only cost about $35, so I always change them.*

### Bearing Retainers

Check for wear on the front bearing retainer's outside collar. It should be smooth with no grooves. A gasket is necessary to maintain the gap between the retainer and case. If no gasket is used it is common to see the retainer develop cracks along the bolt edges. This happens because the retainer is bending around the front bearing since no gasket is there to support it.

## Gears, Synchros and Shafts

Low oil level is the most common cause of premature synchro wear, gear wear, and component failure. These transmissions do not have dipsticks and oil levels are rarely checked; oil changes are often neglected. Because there are no filters the only way to maintain clean oil is to change it.

You should change oil after 200 miles on a fresh rebuild. Silver and bronze particles are always visible in the oil from the new synchros breaking in. Magnets in cases do not attract synchro ring filings or other non-ferrous metals such as those from bushings. After the initial break in, I like to change oil every 10,000 miles.

People often overlook gear wear because they generally don't know how to determine what is acceptable and what isn't. After you clean the parts, look for any galling, pitting, or scuffing of gears. Chipped or broken gear teeth and damaged clutch teeth are usually very obvious.

### Synchronizers

Check for chipped or damaged slider teeth. Sliders that rock excessively on the hubs work but promote excessive fork wear and poor shifting at high RPM. Synchro rings crack at the key slots, flatten, and spin out of the keys. Synchro strut keys, or "dogs," should have clean bumps. If the bumps are worn flat, change them. Hub splines should be even and free from burrs.

*This is an original-equipment GM bearing retainer from the mid-1980s. The input shaft threads rubbed on the inside bore of the retainer because they were not chamfered. This condition caused the unit to lock up when bolting on the retainer. It is a very common issue because many people incorrectly think that purchasing an NOS GM bearing retainer is a good thing.*

*The snap-ring groove often stretches out in the mid-plate. Inspect for cracks on the forward face. If a driveshaft is too long, usually this area cracks open from the driveshaft yoke bottoming out on the transmission's mainshaft; it wants to blow the rear bearing out the front of the midplate. If the locating groove is stretched, the whole output shaft can move back and forth, which crushes the fourth-gear synchro ring and causes falling-out-of-gear issues.*

*This appears to be a fairly clean transmission. It's typical of good wear. The gear teeth have a smooth finish, it is well lubed, and the gear clutch teeth have common wear, which means that they all have a uniform look. They have good point definition and are not chipped or broken. Originally, all Muncies came with a square edge on the 3-4 slider (indicated) and a tapered edge on the 1-2. The taper clears the lower portion of the countergear when the 1-2 slider moves into the second position. Mixing them up causes the square edge to rub against the countergear if it's used on the 1-2.*

*New sliders are tapered and universal. Factory 3-4 sliders also came with torque-locking teeth. Even though this slider's points have some wear, the taper in the spline is actually part of the design. People frequently mistake this as some sort of wear. This taper, or pocket, in the spline prevents the transmission from falling out of gear.*

*Here is a freshly rebuilt transmission that a customer sent to me because of noise in second gear. You can see how the 3-4 slider was placed in the 1-2 position and is hitting the countergear. It's important to recognize the incorrect assembly of a transmission. If you didn't know that it was assembled incorrectly, you would just reassemble it the same way and experience the same problem.*

*Although this transmission appears to be beyond repair, the gears can probably be glass beaded and the synchro cones polished. Until a transmission is completely disassembled, you cannot determine the extent of repairs.*

## Synchro Inspection

### 1 Inspect Synchro Rings

Cracked or damaged synchro rings are easily spotted. However, the height of the ring on the gear cone is what is important and is often overlooked. The left ring has flattened out and no longer grabs the gear. The right ring is at a normal height. Cheap rings balloon open under severe load, so use a good forged bronze ring. Good ring gap is between .040 and .060 inch. This is measured from the rear of the ring to the front face of the clutch teeth.

### 2 Inspect Shift Fork Groove

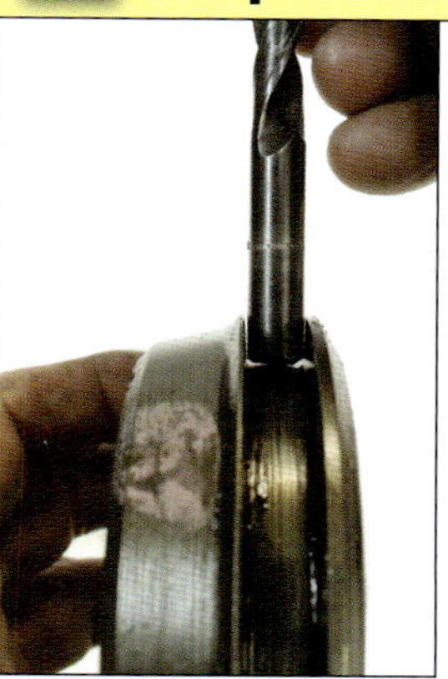
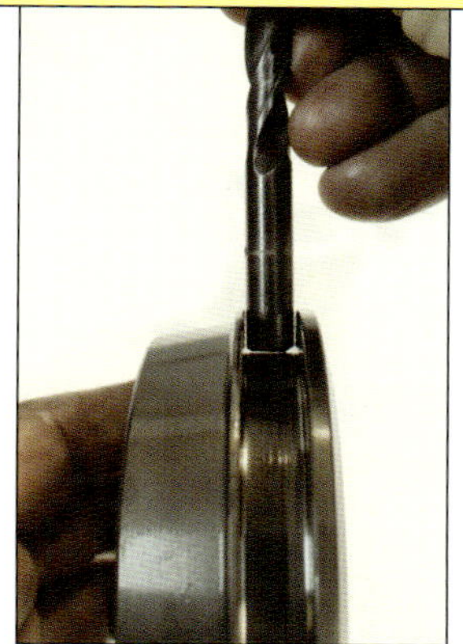

*I checked the shift fork groove of the slider with a 3/8-inch shank of a drill bit. The one on the left has "V"-shaped wear. They are always tight at the bottom and loose at the top. The one on the right is a new slider and both sides of the groove are nicely parallel. Make sure both forks and sliders have nice, flat surfaces.*

### 3 Inspect Slider Teeth

*If your slider teeth are peened over, it causes block-out conditions because the slider can no longer index with the synchro ring. The slider also binds on the hub. If a slider's teeth are mashed over on the second-gear side, the slider cannot move over the hub to get into first. When this happens it may appear to be a first-gear issue when it is actually a second-gear issue.*

### 4 Inspect Hub Splines

When the sides of the hub splines are worn, it causes a shift to hang up because the slider is allowed to cock on the hub. You should always build units with upgraded matching hardened hubs and sliders.

### 5 Inspect Gear Cone

The synchro cone of the gear is often overlooked. This gear is in great shape but the cone has severe groove marks in it from the synchro ring. This happens when oil is dirty and becomes abrasive. The grooves of the new ring may not align with those on the cone and the ring does not grab the gear correctly, which causes intermittent grinds.

*Input and Output Shafts*

Although the input shaft has a gear that also needs to be inspected, think of the input and output shafts as the spine of the transmission. Nothing will work well if they are bent, twisted, or misaligned. Wiggling an input shaft up and down by hand does not determine its integrity.

The input and output shafts float on each other. The pilot bushing in the engine's crankshaft pilots the input shaft. It is held concentric to that bushing by the vehicle's bellhousing. The output shaft is held concentric to the extension housing by the driveshaft's front yoke, which runs on the housing's rear bushing.

If the bellhousing is misaligned to the engine you can get bushing failure at both ends, as well as front bearing failure, and wipe out the mainshaft. If the rear bushing fails the yoke rests on the seal and wipes it out. Rear bushing failure can also cause front bushing failure because that bushing is now overloaded.

## Input and Output Shaft Inspection

### 1 Inspect Pilot Bushing

*The tip of the input shaft goes into the pilot bushing. People often beat on it with a hammer and spread the end open, but then it binds on the pilot. This pilot had some rust on it, so glass beads were used to clean and polish it. A bronze bushing is fine because the full length of the pilot was not damaged.*

### 2 Inspect Shaft

*Older shafts had a tendency to twist under severe load. This spline has twisted, which causes the clutch hub to bind on it. Sometimes the shafts can twist and not have run-out, but in most cases they need to be changed.*

### 3 Check for Excessive Shimming

*This input shaft was over-shimmed and you can see where the front of the mainshaft started to contact the center of the input. I've actually seen instances where both input and output shafts weld themselves together.*

## 4 Check Alignment

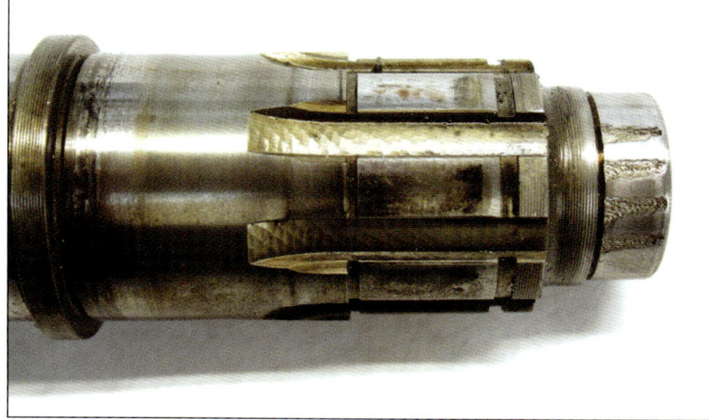

*Misalignment and lack of lubricant caused damage to the front pilot section of this mainshaft. The area in front of the flange got hot and metal started to weld from the gear onto the shaft. Shafts, such as these, can be repaired but new shafts are much better than the old ones and are readily available.*

## 5 Check Oil Circulation

*Performance Tip*

*Here is a mainshaft on which both the third gear and mainshaft started to weld together. It's common on the third-gear section because the oil cannot circulate around the thrust. I grind flats that are 1/4 inch wide, 180 degrees apart, and about .010 inch deep to improve oil flow.*

### Gears

Inspecting the gears thoroughly can give you insight into whether the transmission was properly used, abused, or repaired. When gears break, the tooth fragments get everywhere and usually internal marks are visible in the case from that type of impact damage. Take notice how all the gears look as a whole. Does one gear look different than the others, indicating it was changed? General Motors never numbered gears so look for part numbers on gears, which indicate previous repair.

## Gear Inspection

## 1 Check for Aftermarket Gears

*All factory speed gears were coated with black phosphate (left) and had some sort of inspection dye on them. The inputs and countergears never had these coatings. You can see the coloration difference in an aftermarket gear (right).*

## 2 Inspect Engagement Teeth

*Some aftermarket gears come with torque-locking engagement teeth. This is a stock gear. Its engagement teeth have straight shoulders.*

## 3  Inspect Engagement Teeth
**CONTINUED**

Notice how the teeth on this gear have a back taper to them. You need to use a matching locking slider with such a gear. During on- and off-load conditions, torque-locking teeth are forced to ramp toward the center of the slider, which eliminates gear fall-out issues. You can use locking sliders on non-locking gears, but you cannot use non-locking sliders on locking gears. Therefore, you need to inspect your engagement teeth to determine what type of gears you have. It's common to see these replacement gears in Muncies.

## 4  Remove Rivets

Three rivets fastened an anti-backlash plate to the front of the gear on Muncie M20 clusters. These were used to prevent gear rattle under no-load conditions. However, you must always remove them because the rivets loosen up, plates fall off, and then they do a lot of damage to the case and gears. This outside perimeter is shiny from the 3-4 slider rubbing against the gear. If you have a worn 3-4 fork, the slider can move forward and do this.

## 5  Inspect for Gear Tooth Fatigue

This first-speed section has started to fatigue and the hard surface is damaged. The teeth are starting to twist and crack. This gear needs to be replaced. Check for early signs of pitting. Once it starts it always gets worse.

*Professional Mechanic Tip*

## 6  "Combo-ing Clusters"

When gears were hard to find and very expensive, many rebuilders used this old-school welding fix. It was also a way of changing ratios. You can weld gear sections together if you're a skilled welder. Liberty's Gears did this for years and the process was called "combo-ing clusters."

## 7 Inspect for Broken Gears

Sometimes a broken gear can be ground off and a donor cut off and bored out for a press fit. The two parts are pressed together and then welded.

These are typical examples of blown first-speed gear sections from high-RPM launches. The extremely high RPM impact of a clutch drop basically stripped the teeth completely off first gear.

People who build 3-speed dirt-track transmissions that don't use a first gear recycle them by machining the first-gear section off; they leave just enough for the reverse idler to mesh. I know many rebuilders who have barrels of broken gears for this very reason.

This is a great example of a re-purposed 4-speed counter-gear that can now be used in a racing 3-speed.

## 8 Inspect Thrust Washers and Surfaces

Inspect all thrust washer surfaces for heat cracks and uneven wear. Rub the ends over 400-grit emery paper on a flat surface to smooth these surfaces.

## 9 Determine Gear Wear

*This gear has two problems. The engagement teeth are worn because some point definition is gone and the main teeth are scalloped out in the center (or root) of the gear. A low-lube condition causes gears with this type of wear to make a whining noise.*

## 10 Inspect Clutch Teeth

*This gear has very bad engagement teeth that allow it to fall out of gear. The front bearing is worn, and you can see that heat has discolored the front edge of the teeth because the gear was rubbing on the inside of the case.*

## 11 Inspect Reverse Gear

*Reverse is a non-synchronized gear and is subject to occasional grinding. This idler has a decent chunk taken out of it. The hard surface is gone and when they get like this it's time for a new one. Reverse gears are cheap, so if they are not in great shape, install a new pair in your rebuild.*

*This reverse gear may be chipped on the ends, but once in gear, these ends over-hang the idler and are not in contact, so this gear is still usable.*

## 12 Inspect Speedometer Drivegears

*Speedometer drivegears are always banged up because people do not have a proper puller. These gears are soft, so if you hit them with a hammer or chisel they distort very easily. If your speedometer is jumpy or erratic this is usually the reason. You can dress these teeth with a small triangular file if they have a few dents in them. New gears are approximately $20.*

## Bearings and Bearing Surfaces

NDH made the main ball bearings originally installed in Muncie transmissions. General Motors acquired NDH in 1919 and operated it until 1995, when the doors were finally shut. The Muncie front bearing is currently produced by NTN, KOYO, JAF, BCA (owned by NTN), and a few Chinese companies that seem to repackage under different names. The rear bearing is a standard-size bearing and is available from just about any ball bearing manufacturer.

The specific bearing part numbers installed in Muncies are as follows: front bearings are N307LOE, 1307LOE (max load), and 41307B (max load); rear bearings are 6308NR and 43308NR. You should select the correct bearings for your transmission to maximize performance.

It's important to understand bearing design, how the design affects bearing longevity, and how the wrong bearing can destroy your transmission. Internal clearance between the bearings and the rings is often overlooked.

Clearance is designated with the letter "C" and ranges from C1 to C5. The normal "CN" rating sits between C1 and C2. Automotive gearbox ball bearings require a C3 clearance. This is based on operating speed, oil viscosity, shaft misalignment, and the bearings' ability to pass foreign material through its clearances.

Ford and BorgWarner used bearings with the wrong clearance in Toploaders and T10s in the mid-1970s. This led to premature bearing failure, recalls, and service bulletins that notified dealers to swap out bearings with a new C3 bearing.

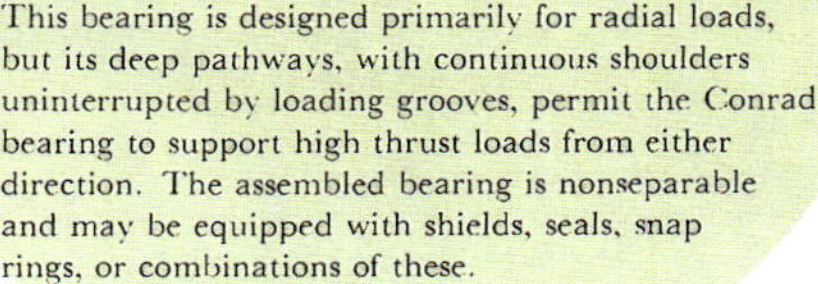



*A description of a Conrad bearing is shown in the original New Departure catalog.*

*This image is also from the New Departure catalog. The product description states that bearing-thrust load is limited when using maximum-capacity-style bearings.*

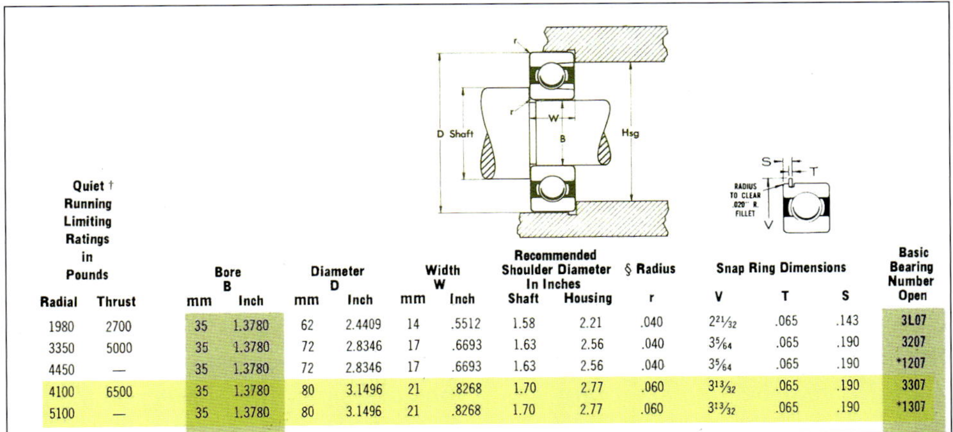



| Quiet † Running Limiting Ratings in Pounds | | Bore B | | Diameter D | | Width W | | Recommended Shoulder Diameter In Inches | | § Radius | Snap Ring Dimensions | | | Basic Bearing Number Open |
|---|---|---|---|---|---|---|---|---|---|---|---|---|---|---|
| Radial | Thrust | mm | Inch | mm | Inch | mm | Inch | Shaft | Housing | r | V | T | S | |
| 1980 | 2700 | 35 | 1.3780 | 62 | 2.4409 | 14 | .5512 | 1.58 | 2.21 | .040 | $2^{21}\!/_{32}$ | .065 | .143 | 3L07 |
| 3350 | 5000 | 35 | 1.3780 | 72 | 2.8346 | 17 | .6693 | 1.63 | 2.56 | .040 | $3^{5}\!/_{64}$ | .065 | .190 | 3207 |
| 4450 | — | 35 | 1.3780 | 72 | 2.8346 | 17 | .6693 | 1.63 | 2.56 | .040 | $3^{5}\!/_{64}$ | .065 | .190 | *1207 |
| 4100 | 6500 | 35 | 1.3780 | 80 | 3.1496 | 21 | .8268 | 1.70 | 2.77 | .060 | $3^{13}\!/_{32}$ | .065 | .190 | 3307 |
| 5100 | — | 35 | 1.3780 | 80 | 3.1496 | 21 | .8268 | 1.70 | 2.77 | .060 | $3^{13}\!/_{32}$ | .065 | .190 | *1307 |

*You can see in this bearing ratings chart from New Departure that the maximum-capacity bearing 1307 has no thrust-load rating compared to the standard 3307 bearing.*

### Types of Bearings

Many companies are selling maximum-capacity bearings containing more balls. These are not really good bearings to use in a Muncie.

*I've lined up the filling slot on the 12-ball maximum-capacity BCA bearing on the right. An 8-ball bearing from Koyo is on the left. Muncie gears have a helix angle to them, so the maximum-capacity bearing cannot properly absorb the thrust load. If you use spur-type gears, the maximum-capacity bearing is a better choice.*

*Although technically not a bearing, this is a factory first-gear sleeve (or bushing). The valley in the center of the sleeve is a normal place for oil to collect. Most people think they are worn. The rear-bearing inner ring presses against this sleeve, which allows the first gear to thrust against the 1-2 synchro hub and the rear bearing's inner ring.*

The 307-series bearing is almost the same as the bearing used in the Muncie. The 3307 is the standard Conrad style and the 1307 is the maximum capacity style, which has no thrust rating.

*This is an original maximum-capacity NDH 41307B. This bearing only has 11 balls. The extra ball creates unneeded friction, heat, and reduced thrust load.*

*Sealed ball bearings are used in most modern transmissions. The seals keep dirt and debris out of the bearing, prolonging bearing life. Dirt contamination is the number-one cause of bearing failure. When choosing a rear bearing, make sure that the inner ring has a wide enough surface for the first gear to thrust against; this is a common oversight. The bearing on the left, from SKF, works. The other bearing on the right, made in Turkey, allows first gear to thrust against the bearing's seal and locks up the transmission.*

*Another issue with many capacity bearings is that the separator cage drops onto the inner race and comes apart. This happens because of the excessive heat generated by having more balls. Notice the damaged front nut from a poor installation.*

*You must properly prep and examine the bearing to determine its health. People spin bearings by hand and think they are worn out if they "feel" noisy. Shop dust makes a bearing spin "notchy." Washing a bearing in a parts washer also gives you the same effect. That doesn't mean it is bad. You need to thoroughly clean the bearing, blow it out with air, and then oil it to see if it quiets down. Use a high-powered LED flashlight to inspect the bearing and look for pits. Here, I cut away some races to show the difference between a good used bearing (left) and one that had extreme spalling and surface fatigue (right).*

# REBUILDING YOUR MUNCIE

*Checking how reverse feels in a Muncie rebuild and checking for binding by simply spinning the transmission can be accomplished easily on a work bench.*

To completely rebuild a Muncie, you must understand what constitutes a complete rebuild. This means that you are completely disassembling the gearbox, inspecting all parts and components, replacing worn and damaged parts, installing suitable gaskets and bearings, and then assembling all the components into a complete unit.

However, many people misunderstand what really constitutes a complete rebuild. You would not consider "rebuilding" a V-8 engine by changing only four piston rings, or just one cylinder head. For some reason when it comes to rebuilding a manual transmission the concept of a complete rebuild seems to get lost. Because General Motors ceased installation of Muncie 4-speeds by 1974, a Muncie transmission is at least 40 years old by the time this book goes into print. Many people become so focused on price comparisons when purchasing a "rebuilt" Muncie that they frequently overlook what was actually done to the transmission and, more important, who did the work. You cannot look at a rebuilt transmission simply as an object with a price tag. Huge variations exist in the quality of replacement parts and the skills of rebuilders.

By 1981 I had developed the first retail rebuild kit for the Muncie. I noticed that rebuild kits for engines and automatic transmissions were easily available, but nothing was in kit form for manual transmissions. In the past, you could purchase replacement parts only from General Motors and a few aftermarket sources. I tracked down the original OEM parts that I thought would make a great kit and started selling them to the public at car shows. Many people have copied my idea, yet I still have sold thousands of kits. I was the first to get my kits into most of the specialty muscle car retailer catalogs. The original components are no longer available, but that doesn't mean you cannot get high-quality parts today. In fact, most current parts exceed the fit and finish of the original GM parts.

Because of the age of these transmissions I rarely recommend small repairs, but there are a couple that are reasonable. The most common small repair is to change the front bearing retainer. Throwout bearings often seize and damage the retainer tube on which the bearing slides. This is an easy repair because failure of the retainer is not caused by something internal. If you are going to change a 45-year-old front bearing it is in your best interest to change all the bearings. Another common repair is a rear seal change.

I have two classifications of parts for Muncies: hard and soft. Soft parts are included in a rebuild kit but hard parts are not.

## Muncie Rebuild Kit

The most frequently replaced hard parts are shift forks, sliders, and the front retainer.

Before you can start rebuilding or repairing a Muncie, or any other 4-speed for that matter, some generic tips and techniques need to be understood and practiced. I have developed these during my 30-plus years in this line of work. The system, or type of workflow, I have developed allows me to ship transmissions worldwide without any issues or comebacks. I spend most of my time building new transmissions with all-new parts. It can never be taken for granted that the installation of new parts guarantees a fully functional and problem-free unit.

*This is the Muncie kit I designed and have sold for more than 30 years. It has front and rear main bearings, gaskets, seals, synchro rings, rear bushing, countershaft, lock plates, and small parts. Small parts include needle bearings, snap rings, thrust washers, needle spacers, front nut, oil slinger, reverse detent spring, reverse detent ball, strut keys, and strut key springs.*

## Workflow Process

Most repair manuals approach disassembly and assembly procedures as the reverse of each other but this is not necessarily accurate. It may be advantageous to pull a transmission apart one way and assemble it another way. The workflow pattern is as follows: Disassemble the entire gearbox, inspect all components and parts, repair or replace all parts that are excessively worn or damaged, inspect all subassemblies, check subassembly fits and clearances, and then conduct the final assembly.

### Disassembly

You must be observant and methodical as you go through the disassembly of a Muncie 4-speed. Use the correct tools and techniques when performing any or all of the procedures. When I begin disassembly of a transmission, the first thing I do is visually inspect the transmission for broken bolts, cracked castings, oversize bolts that com-

## Muncie Rebuild Kit Components

- Front and rear main bearings
- Four forged bronze synchronizer rings
- All gaskets and seals
- Front bearing nut
- Oil slinger
- Extension housing bushing
- Front retainer lock plates

- Countershaft
- Strut keys and springs
- Small parts: needle bearings, snap rings, all thrust washers, roll pins, tapered reverse pin, speedo clip, needle bearing spacer rings
- Reverse detent ball and spring

## Basic Hand Tools for a Muncie Rebuild

- Snap-ring pliers
- Pry bar
- Hammer
- 1/2-, 9/16-, 5/8-inch sockets and combination wrenches
- Adjustable wrench or 8-point 9/16 socket for fill plugs and drain plugs
- Torque wrench
- Assembly lube (heavy wheel-bearing grease can be used)
- Permatex 51813 sealant
- Hydraulic press
- Propane torch
- Chisel and hammer
- Knife and steel wool to remove gaskets

pensate for stripped threads, signs of oil leakage, and paint. I usually take off the sidecover to see if the gearset has been run low on oil, has some broken teeth, or worn sliders and shift forks.

Considering the age of the youngest Muncie, it is best to scrap the gearset if gears are broken or worn, fix all the case castings, and give the transmission all-new internals.

Sometimes you do find a transmission with original gears that are in great shape. That's the type of transmission I used for this build.

*A Dremel or rotary tool is helpful for deburring gears. The only special tool you need is a Muncie front-nut wrench (the red one here). You can use a pipe wrench if you are careful.*

*Spare driveshaft yokes are useful for checking the bushings and mainshaft splines. Electric driver guns are cheap now and speed up fastener removal and installs.*

## Muncie Disassembly

### 1  Remove Sidecover Bolts

Start by placing the 1-2 shifter shaft in the second-gear position. Then remove the seven 1/2-inch-head 5/16-13 threaded bolts.

### 2  Remove Sidecover

The sidecover alignment dowel is located below the upper right bolt. Pry near the dowel to remove the cover. You will disassemble it later.

### 3  Remove Front Bearing Retainer

This transmission had no lock plates, but usually you would bend the lock tabs away from the bolts and remove the four 9/16-inch-head 3/8-16 bolts. Early units had a 1/2-inch head.

*Professional Mechanic Tip*

## 4 | Remove Mainshaft Nut

**PRO TIP** *Most front nuts are seized onto the shaft. Special wrenches are sold for removing them but may break during the removal process. They are soft steel and are left-hand threaded. You can use a chisel to easily remove them. New nuts are cheap. U.S.-made nuts have a better thread-fit than nuts made in China.*

## 5 | Remove Lock Pin

*The reverse shifter shaft lock pin is a No. 0 tapered pin that is wider at the top than at the bottom. You have to remove this pin from the bottom. Most are also seized, and you may need to apply heat with a propane torch in this area to knock it out.*

## 6 | Tap Out Shifter Shaft

*Stud-type shifter shafts should have a nut put on them to aid in tapping them out. Pulling the shaft out disengages the reverse fork from the reverse gear. Use a 3/8-16 bolt as a tap surface for bolt-on shafts.*

## 7 | Remove Speedometer Drive Fitting

*Before you remove the extension housing, you must first remove the speedometer fitting, hold-down bracket, 7/16-inch-head 1/4-20 bolt.*

## 8  Remove Tail Section Bolts

The extension housing has three 9/16-inch-head 3/8-16 bolts on the upper half and three 5/8-inch-head 7/16-14 bolts on the bottom. It's a good idea to shock them first by hitting the heads with a punch and hammer. The factory never used lock washers and they are often seized and break.

## 9  Separate Tail from Main Case

Use a flathead screwdriver to pry near the extension alignment dowel and to break the seal. Be careful because you don't want to damage the mating surfaces. Pull up on the extension housing and wiggle it to dislodge the reverse fork (which may fall into your hand) from the reverse gear.

## 10  Remove Reverse Idler Gear

Pry under the reverse idler gear to remove the gear, thrust washer, and idler shaft. Don't force it; gently work it loose. Sometimes the shaft may be stuck in the extension housing. If so, remove it from the extension.

## 11  Remove Thrust Washer

Simply lift the forward reverse idler and thrust washer from the case.

## 12 Remove Gears from Case

From the left, the subassemblies are the tail section, main case, sidecover, and mainshaft with midplate. Focus on getting all the gears removed and then disassemble the sidecover and extension housing.

## 13 Remove Input-Shaft Bearing Cage and Needle Bearings

Remove the input-shaft bearing cage and lift out the 17 needles. New needles are in small parts and rebuild kits, but the cages are not. Usually they end up in the bottom of the case.

*Special Tool*

## 14 Remove Outer Snap Ring

Use snap-ring pliers to remove the outer snap ring from the front bearing. Sometimes you can pry on this and remove the bearing. This one is really tight and will have to be pressed off.

## 15 Remove Countershaft from Case

Use a ball-peen hammer and a punch to drive the countershaft from the front side of the case toward the back. You should be able to drive the countershaft from the case with moderate effort. Muncies are rarely tight enough to need a press. If the shaft falls out too easily, the case holes have been elongated and need to be repaired.

## 16 Slide Countershaft Back

Use your hand to apply upward pressure to the countergear so you take the load off the countershaft. You can pull the shaft out of the back of the case, and then safely store it.

## 17 Remove Maindrive Shaft

Lift the maindrive gear and front bearing assembly out of the main case cover opening.

## 18 Remove Countergear

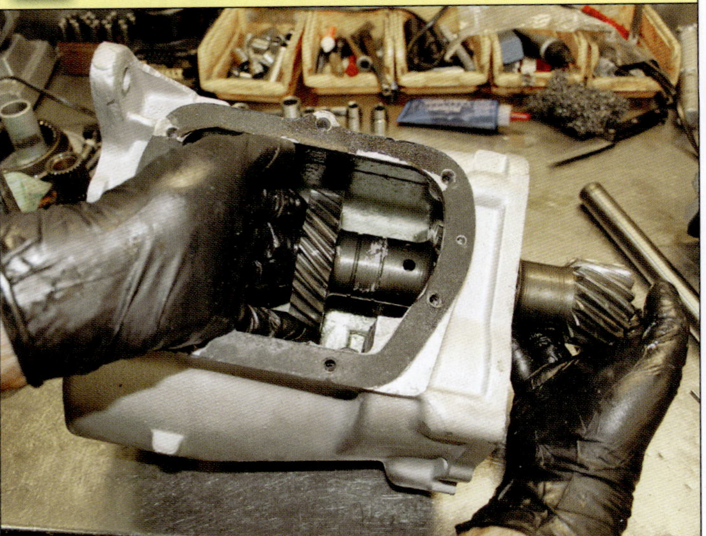

Lift the countergear out of the case. If the case was damaged from a gear explosion, the thrust washers are often jammed from debris. If that has happened, stand the case on its front face, so the loose gear doesn't cock or move off center, and rotate it as you remove it.

## 19 Remove Needle Bearings

*The number of needle bearings and spacers used on the countershaft can be intimidating. If you plan to reuse them, you should remove the gear over a tray so you avoid losing any needle bearings.*

## 20 Remove Front Bearing

*Special Tool*

*Use an arbor press to remove the front bearing. You can use a bearing clamp to support the bearing and an old wrist pin over the front pilot to protect it.*

## 21 Remove Front Bearing Option

*You can also use the "non-press" or manual method to remove the front bearing. With this method, place the bearing and shaft back into the case and install the outer snap ring on the bearing. Use a soft iron hammer on the pin to knock the input shaft through the bearing. Never strike the input shaft itself.*

### Mainshaft Disassembly

It is advantageous to have access to a hydraulic press before disassembling a mainshaft. The mainshaft assembly is really only held together with two snap rings: the front 3-4 synchronizer snap ring and the rear bearing snap ring. Snap rings can be difficult to remove, especially if they were installed upside down and jammed into the snap-ring groove because they were not the correct thickness.

Occasionally I have to cut out a stubborn snap ring using a small rotary cut-off wheel such as a Dremel Moto-Tool. Never use a hammer as a substitute for a press. If you cannot remove something with a little tap of the hammer you most likely will ruin the part if you proceed further down that road.

## Mainshaft Disassembly

### 1. Remove 3-4 Synchro Snap Ring

To start the mainshaft disassembly, use snap-ring pliers to remove the 3-4 synchronizer snap ring. The 3-4 slider and keys fell out when I removed the mainshaft.

*Professional Mechanic Tip* **PRO TIP**

### 2. Remove 3-4 Synchro Hub

**PRO TIP** *Usually the gear and 3-4 synchro hub dislodge if you hold third gear and gently tap on the front of the mainshaft. Later units have hardened hubs with extremely tight press fits, and you must use a press to remove them. If the gear and hub do not come off, do not use a hammer to try to remove them. The tip of the mainshaft is easily damaged. You need to use a press and bearing clamp on third gear for removal.*

### 3. Remove Speedometer Gear

Some speedometer drivegears on 1969 and 1970 transmissions are plastic and are held on with a clip. Obviously, those are easily removed. Steel gears should always replace the plastic gears. The steel gears are soft and pullers easily damage them. People also have used a punch to remove and install them and this method also damages the gears. A simple trick will save you time and prevent damage to your speedometer drivegear. Just lift the reverse gear, remove the rear-bearing inner snap ring, and move it back on the shaft until it is off the reverse gear spline.

### 4. Press off Mainshaft Gears

Second gear is supporting the geartrain during this mainshaft press procedure. Press the mainshaft through the complete assembly all in one shot. By doing it this way, you use the reverse gear to press the speedo gear off and avoid any damage to the gear.

## 5 Slide Gears and Parts off Mainshaft

First and second gear, the 1-2 synchro assembly, first-gear sleeve, reverse gear, speedometer gear, and the rear bearing midplate slide off the shaft together.

## 7 Remove Shift Forks from Sidecover

Pull both the 3-4 and 1-2 forks out of the sidecover. If you think you are going to reuse them, mark the position and orientation of each fork so they can be reinstalled in the exact position. I typically replace the forks because most are worn, and they are just too old.

## 6 Remove Rear Bearing

Use snap-ring pliers to spread the rear bearing retaining ring open and then tap the bearing with a hammer to dislodge it from the ring. Light tapping should drive the bearing out of the bore. At this point, the geartrain is completely apart.

*Documentation Required*

## 8 Remove Shifter Shafts

Remove both shift levers and mark them so they can be replaced in the same bores. It's a good idea to make a note if they wobble in the bore. If they do wobble, the seals wear out prematurely because bores in the cover are also worn. This means that you should also replace the cover.

*Sidecover Disassembly and Rebuild*

Some people never disassemble the sidecover when doing a rebuild. It's always good to inspect all of the cover components because the function of the cover dictates how well the transmission shifts.

## Sidecover Disassembly

### 1 Remove Spring

Notice the positions of the cams and the spring. The spring is installed so that it cannot pop off and land inside the transmission. Always reinstall the spring facing in this direction. I always replace these with a 20-pound cover spring.

### 2 Pry off C-Clip

Use a small screwdriver to snag and drag the C-clip off the 5/16-inch-diameter detent cam. Put your other hand over the C-clip to catch it once it clears the cam. These have a tendency to fly off the cover and get lost. Once the clip is off, remove the cams.

## Tail Housing and Sidecover Rebuild

### 1 Lightly File Midplate Gasket Surfaces

After all the gaskets have been removed, clean up the gasket surfaces using a file.

### 2 Preassemble Base Components

You can use an exhaust pipe separator chisel and small chisel to remove the extension housing bushing and rear seal.

## 3 Remove Rear Seal

I use a chisel that I have sharpened to remove the rear seal. Catch the edge of the seal with the chisel and punch it out. Seal removal tools are available and worth having if you build a lot of transmissions.

## 4 Remove Tail Housing Bushing

Place the exhaust pipe separator chisel in the oil return slot. It cuts a nice slot in the bushing when you hit it with a hammer.

*Critical Inspection*

## 5 Inspect Tail Housing Section

Once you have adequately tapped on the bushing, the bushing drops right out. Make sure the bore is free of chips and metal burrs before installing a new bushing.

## 6 Pry Shifter Shaft Seals from Sidecover

Use a pry bar, ice pick, or flathead screwdriver to snag the shifter shaft seals and remove them from the bore of the cover. Be careful not to damage the bore.

## 7 Coat Shifter Pin

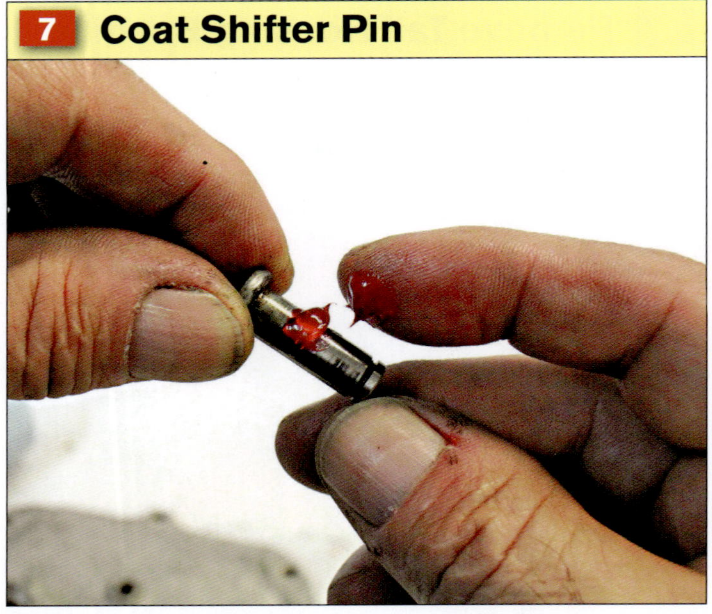

*This cover pivot pin was loose, so I coated it with Permatex 51813. This acts like a sealant and a threadlocking compound. If the pin is really loose, replace the cover.*

## 8 Seal Pivot Pin

*Within 10 minutes the pin is locked and sealed in place. Wipe away any excess sealant.*

## 9 Inspect Combs for Straightness

*The combs must be flat. Check that they are flush against each other. Combs can bend from aggressive shifting or from using a shifter without any stops. New combs are harder and much better than the older ones. If they are really bad you should change them out.*

## 10 Straighten Combs

*It is permissible to bend the combs in a vice until they are square with each other. Check for any nicks and deburr all rough edges. If the combs are bent they do not run along each other smoothly.*

## 11 Install Detent Combs

Combs have a rounded side and a flat side. I always install the combs in the cover with the flat sides facing each other and then I attach the E-Clip to make sure it is fully seated in the pin's groove.

## 12 Install Sidecover Spring

I use a 20-pound spring. Use pliers or a spring hook to install the spring. Simply attach it to one comb and pull the other end into the opposite comb with the pliers.

## 13 Tap in Sidecover Seals

I coat the outer edges of the sidecover seal with Permatex 51813. I use the case to support the cover when I press in the sidecover seals with a 17-mm socket. Make sure the seal is square in the bore and that you drive it in evenly. These seals seat in the bore with light taps.

## 14 Install Shift Shafts

Apply assembly lube to the shifter shafts and install them in the cover. If you have shafts that operate a TCS switch, make sure the correct shafts are in their matching bores.

## 15 Install Shift Forks

Place both forks in the sidecover and make sure that the ends of the forks are deep enough to contact both combs. Place the cover in the second-gear position.

***Tail Housing Rebuild***

Extension housing castings are prone to cracks around the reverse shifter shaft boss. The shifter mounting plate and transmission mount bolt holes usually have stripped threads or seized bolts. Try to be patient when you come across these rebuilding obstacles. Invest in the proper thread repair kits and seek out quality weld repair work if it becomes necessary.

## Tail Housing Rebuild

### 1  File Bushing

*Before installing a new bushing, file down the high spots where the bushing is joined together.*

### 2  Install Bushing

*Special Tool*

*Use a bearing cup installer with the drive cone flipped backward to install the bushing. Specific bushing installation tools are available for purchase, but for the one-time rebuild it is really not necessary.*

### 3  Check Bushing Clearances

*Sometimes you can spread the bushing end. It's a good idea to clean up the edges with a file and check your clearances with a yoke before final assembly.*

### 4  Install Spring and Detent Ball

*Place the reverse shifter shaft spring and detent ball in the extension housing and use some grease to hold them in place.*

## 5 Install Reverse Shifter Shaft

Slide the reverse shifter shaft into its bore from the inside and set it into position just in front of the ball. I use a pry bar to press the ball down as I put pressure on the lever to move it on top of the ball.

## 6 Check Reverse Arm Position

Be careful not to go too far or the ball pops out. It's best to position the reverse arm midway.

## 7 Install Reverse Shifter Shaft Seal

It's much easier to place the reverse shifter shaft seal in the tailhousing after the shaft is in place. The seal presses against a step within the bore. It cannot go any farther.

## 8 Grease Rear Seal

Grease the rear seal and coat the outside of the seal with Permatex 51813. Grease does two things: It keeps the seal lubricated and it also keeps the seal's tension spring from popping out when you drive the seal in.

## 9 | Seat Rear Seal

*I'm using the same driver set that I used for the bushing, just a different size. Flip the driver upside down and gently tap in the seal until it is seated.*

## 10 | Clean Up

*Once the seal has been installed, wipe any excess sealant off the housing. It helps make your rebuild look more professional.*

### Mainshaft Assembly

Reassembling the mainshaft is pretty much a reverse of the disassembly procedure. Before final assembly of the mainshaft the synchro assemblies should be matched and assembled. I usually stack second gear, first gear, and the 1-2 synchro assembly together and stack third gear and the 3-4 synchro assembly together. The midplate is preassembled with the rear bearing.

Having all these subassemblies ready to go on the mainshaft helps to keep you organized.

# Prepare Hub and Slider Assemblies

## 1 | Position Synchro Hubs

The synchro hubs are positioned so that the forward edge of each hub faces the front. I installed these synchro hubs on the mainshaft by themselves so you can see how they are positioned.

*Important!*

## 2 | Double-Check Parts Orientation

*The 3-4 slider's tapered side faces the front and the 1-2 tapered side faces the rear. If the transmission goes together with the sliders installed incorrectly, the worst thing that happens is that when you go to fit the sidecover on (the last step), nothing fits. The orientation of these parts is critical.*

### 3  Set Up Gear Synchronizers

*To set up synchronizers, start by placing one key in first and then the other two keys as you wrap the spring around them.*

### 4  Install Spring

*Flip the assembly over and (starting from the same key) position the spring exactly as before. Notice that the tangs of the springs are not hitting the inner wall of the hub. You can grind down the tang down if it does.*

## Speedometer Gear Calculations

I've seen many people frustrated because they took the time to do a thorough job rebuilding a used Muncie, but later, after the transmission is installed, they find out that the speedometer is reading incorrectly. When I build a new transmission or do a rebuild, I always ask the customer these four questions:

What is the tire size you plan to use? (Example: 255/60/15)
If you don't know the tire size, do you know the diameter?
What is the axle ratio?
Do you know the tooth count of the speedometer drive gear in the transmission?

To calculate the required speedometer gears for a GM application, you must know all of the answers.

### Formula for Calculating Tire Diameter

Using the example above, 255/60/15 means that the tire has a section width of 255 mm. It has an aspect ratio of 60, which is the ratio of sidewall height to section width. The final number, 15, is the actual wheel diameter.

Here's the formula for calculating tire diameter:

Tire Diameter = (2 x sidewall height) + wheel diameter

First you have to convert the section width to inches. You, divide it by 25.4. In our example:

Section Width = 255 mm ÷ 25.4 = 10 inches

Next, you find the sidewall height. You multiply the section width by the aspect ratio. In our example:

Sidewall Height = 10 x .60 = 6 inches

Using the formula, our example tire diameter is 27 inches.

(6 x 2) + 15 = 27 inches

# Speedometer Gear Calculations *CONTINUED*

## Formula for Calculating Speedometer Driven Teeth

Driven-Gear Tooth Count = (speedo drive-gear tooth count x axle ratio x tire revs per mile) ÷ 1,001

The formula to calculate tire revolutions per mile is:

Tire Revs Per Mile = 20,168 ÷ tire diameter (inches)

Using the tire example above:

$$20{,}168 \div 27 = 747 \text{ revs per mile}$$

Before calculating the driven-gear tooth count, the drive-gear tooth count must be determined.

Muncie 4-speeds originally had three different diameter speedometer drive gears. The six-tooth gear (no longer available) had no driven-gear options except for one steel 20T pencil gear.

The parts resource guide lists two major diameter drive gears: 1.76 and 1.84 inches.

Driven pencil gears come in tooth count ranges that coincide with the size of the drive gear.

General Motors discontinued the 1.76-inch drive gears and the corresponding driven gears. Because the 1.84-inch diameter was used in automatics, the cable-threaded fittings and driven pencil gears have been reproduced. AGE makes additional 7- and 9-tooth gears to work with these standardized pencil gears. It is now possible to calibrate your speedometer for a wider combination of rear axle and tire sizes.

So, if you have an eight-tooth drive gear and use the above equation with an axle ratio of 3.73:1 you get 22:

$$(8 \times 3.73 \times 747) \div 1{,}001 = 22$$

If you use a large-diameter eight-tooth gear, you may want to switch to a seven-tooth gear. In this case you get 19 or 20 (depending on how you "round" the answer):

$$(7 \times 3.73 \times 747) \div 1001 = 19.48$$

Because a seven-tooth 1.84-inch-diameter gear is now available, using one puts you more in the middle range of driven pencil gears; it also gives you more options. ■

*These are the drive gears. From left to right: 1.84-inch 32-spline output shaft, 1.84-inch 27-spline output shaft, and 1.76-inch 27-spline output shaft.*

*The drive-gear's tooth count is determined by laying the gear on its side and marking where each spiral-worm tooth comes to an end. This gear has eight teeth and is 1.76 inches in diameter.*

Notice that the diameter of the blue gear is smaller than that of the yellow gear. Small-diameter pencils work with 1.84-inch drive gears; the range is 17 to 22 teeth. Large-diameter pencils work with 1.76-inch drive gears; the range is 22 to 25 teeth.

Most 1969–1970 Muncies came with an eight-tooth plastic drive gear and clip. These do not fit well on the shaft. If your cable or speedometer locks up, the clip breaks, and the gear becomes dislodged; this requires transmission removal and partial disassembly. It is the same diameter as a 1.84-inch steel gear. Always upgrade to a steel drive gear if you are doing a rebuild.

## Mainshaft Assembly

### 1 Install Rear Bearing

Install the rear bearing. Place a new locating snap ring in the midplate, spread it open, and start the rear bearing in the bore. Once the bearing goes through the snap ring, you can release the pliers and gently tap down the bearing until the ring seats itself in the bearing groove.

### 2 Install 1-2 Synchro Assembly

Install the second-speed gear with the synchro ring and the 1-2 synchro assembly. Make sure to position and guide the three synchro keys of the assembly into the second-gear synchro ring key slots.

## 3 Install First-Gear Bushing on Mainshaft

*Performance Tip*

*Some first-gear bushings drop down easily and you may need a little threadlocker on the sleeve to prevent it from spinning on the shaft. Others require a press. This one tapped gently into place. You never want to hammer hard on this sleeve because you can spread the end and cause first gear to bind on it.*

## 4 Install First Gear

*Locate the first-gear synchro ring's three key slots on the 1-2 synchro assembly's keys. Install first gear with a little oil in its bore.*

## 5 Tap Down Midplate

*Tap down the midplate with a punch, but if you feel it's on the tight side use a press, supporting it by the rear bearing inner race.*

## 6 Install Rear Snap Ring

*Small parts kits usually have three selective-fit rear snap rings. The object is to get the thickest ring in the rear mainshaft snap-ring groove. Fit the thickest ring you can into the groove using snap-ring pliers.*

*Precision Measurement*

## 7 Measure and Install Snap Ring

*If you don't have a micrometer you can try to fit the ring by eye. I use a micrometer because some rings only vary in thickness by .005 inch. Different kits come with different ring sizes varying from .078 to .101 inch.*

## 8 Install Reverse Gear

*Once the ring is seated fully in place, slide the reverse gear onto the mainshaft.*

## 9 Remove Anti-Rattle Springs

*Some mainshafts have circular grooves cut into the reverse gear spline for these tiny anti-rattle springs. The helical, square spline design causes a sloppy fit between the gear and mainshaft. The circular springs keep tension on the gear to prevent rattles. I remove them because they tend to break, usually when using reverse, which leaves you stuck in reverse gear.*

## 10 Install Speedo Drivegear

*Heat the speedo drivegear with a propane torch and slide it onto place.*

## 11 Position Speedometer Gear on Mainshaft

*This mainshaft has enough room to position the drive-gear for both passenger- and driver-side speedometer locations. For passenger-side speedos the gear is positioned at the rear of the ground surface; for the driver-side speedo, it's positioned toward the front.*

## 12 Install Third Gear and Synchro Ring

*Place third gear and its synchro ring on the mainshaft. Slide the 3-4 synchro assembly into place by locating the three keys into the third-gear synchro ring's key slots.*

## 13 Install 3-4 Gear Snap Ring

*Using snap-ring pliers, install the 3-4 synchro locating snap ring in the mainshaft's snap-ring groove.*

## 14 Set Aside Mainshaft Assembly

*Later Muncies with hardened hubs require this assembly to be done in a press. This is not model or year specific. If you had to press the hubs off, you most likely have to press them back on. Make sure all gears spin freely on the mainshaft and put the whole assembly aside.*

# Needle Bearing Installation in Countergear

## 1 Load Needle Bearings

Loading all needle bearings is the job everyone hates because it's tedious work. In this case, you're loading 112 needle bearings. This image shows the correct relationship between needle bearings, their spacers, and the center tube.

**BONUS CONTENT**

**How to Rebuild a Muncie 4-Speed (Installing Needle Bearings)**

Scan this QR code with your smartphone to view a video that shows how the author approaches installing Muncie 4-speed countergear needle bearings.

## 3 Insert Spacer Tube in Countergear Shaft

Start by using plenty of grease and insert the spacer tube. I use an assembly lube specifically for transmissions. It remains tacky even when the air temperature is high.

## 2 Determine Number of Needle Spacers

*Important!*

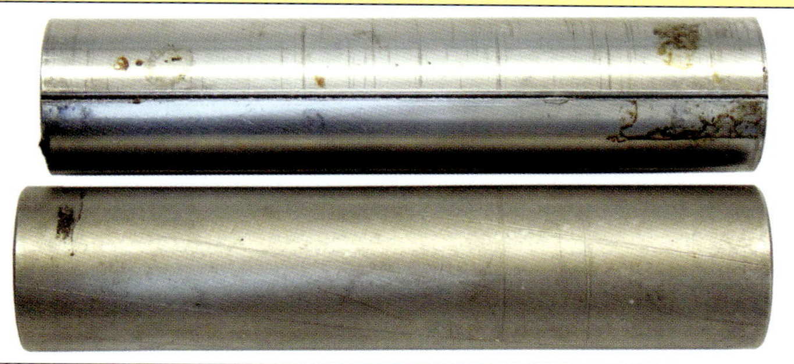

If you have a split-seam tube always use six needle spacers. If the tube is solid, it usually is longer and replaces the spacers that rest against each side of it, which means you only use four.

## 4 Load Countergear Needles

With the spacer tube in place, load the split-seam tube. Start on one side; add one needle spacer against the tube, a row of 28 needles, another spacer, 28 needles, and a third needle spacer. Apply as much lube as necessary to hold the needles in place.

## 5 | Test Countershaft Fit with Needles

Flip the gear over and repeat the process in step 4. Never use a dummy shaft to load needles. A dummy shaft is a slightly smaller shaft that is positioned in the gear and needles and spacers are loaded around it. You place the gear in the transmission with this shaft and then use the good shaft to push out the dummy shaft. I always say, "Dummy shafts are for dummies." You have no final visual with a dummy shaft. I run the actual countershaft that I will use through the countergear outside the transmission so that I can feel for any high spots, possible binding, or a bent shaft. Simply hold the front needles in with your left hand and push the shaft through with your right. Pull the shaft out and it packs the needles for you.

## 6 | Inspect Packed Needle Bearings

Once you remove the shaft you get a great view of the packed needles. This is something that you cannot do with the dummy shaft method.

## 7 | Check Needle Bearing Space

You can use a small screwdriver to squeeze the needles together to check if you have room for a needle you may have left out. Again, this is something you cannot do with a dummy shaft.

## Oil Slinger Installation

## 1 | Install Oil Slinger on Input Shaft

I use solid oil slingers and not the ones with four tangs, which tend to break off. A solid slinger is on the shaft (left) and I'm holding a tanged slinger (right).

## 2 | Install Front Bearing

Place the slinger on the input shaft and tap on the front bearing. Notice the way I'm gripping the punch while tapping the bearing. I drive it straight down the shaft until it's seated. I've also used a press for ones that have a really tight fit. If you have to press it on, support the bearing by the inner race and press the input shaft into it.

## 3 Trial Fit Main Drive Assembly in Case

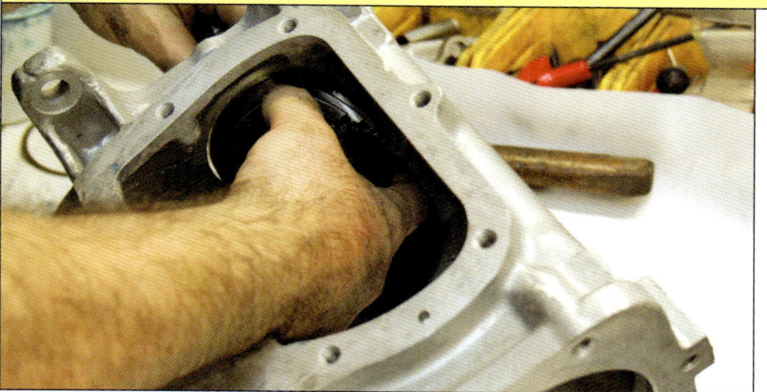

*Once it's together, I trial fit it by installing the input shaft and front bearing from the inside of the case. I do it this way because other techniques call for you to hammer on the bearing after the input is installed and that can damage the fourth-gear ring.*

# Main Section Assembly

## 1 Install Bearing Assembly into Input Shaft

*Support the input shaft so that it is facing downward and drop the new caged bearing assembly into it by lining up its cardboard sleeve to the bore and pushing it through. If you are reusing your old cage, hold the needles in place with grease on the outside perimeter of the cage and gently push it into place.*

*Professional Mechanic Tip*

## 2 Install Front Thrust Washer

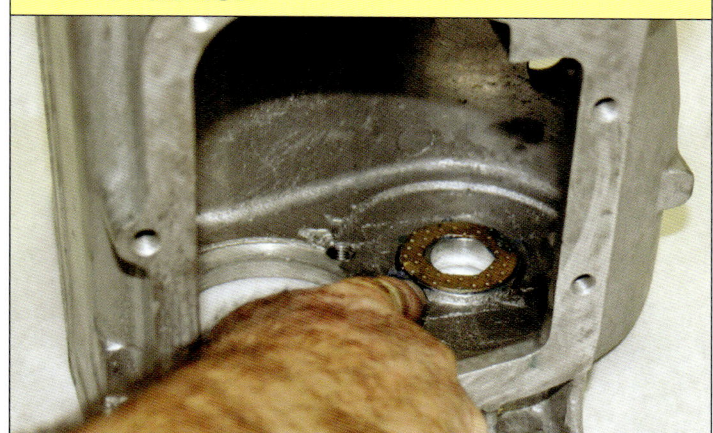

*Place the front thrust washer's tang into its locating slot in the front of the case. I use grease to hold it in place.*

## 3 Place Countergear on Thrust Washer

*Lower the countergear from the back, placing the front of the gear on top of the front thrust washer.*

## 4 Install Rear Thrust Washer

*Install the rear washer and push the whole countergear to the bottom of the case. Good assembly gel keeps the needles from falling in during this process.*

## 5 Place Input Shaft in Case

*Install the input shaft assembly from the inside of the case. The countergear is still dropped to allow it to be placed in this position.*

## 6 Install and Position Countergear and Shaft

*Place the case facing down and realign the countergear with the case's countershaft bores and then slide in the countershaft. Make sure it clears the front thrust washer and seats in the front bore.*

## 7 Drive Countershaft into Bores

*This case has the counter-shaft bores realigned and bushed. If you are reusing a case with a stock bore, use 51813 Permatex to coat the front bore and rear of the shaft. Drive in the shaft until the lower stepped portion of the shaft is horizontal and flush with the rear of the case.*

## 8 Prep Gears for Assembly

*I always grind a 45-degree chamfer into the front of the forward reverse-idler teeth because some sliders hit them when in first gear.*

## 9 Remove Burrs from Gears

*Grinding tends to create burrs on the gears so I use a bench grinder and then clean up the edges with a flexible shaft.*

## 11 Coat Midplate with Gasket Sealant

A transmission that leaks after a rebuild can be a huge disappointment. (I never have leaks.) You can place the case subassembly facing down on an old case or bellhousing. I use a skin coat of 51813 Permatex sealant on the case.



Position the 3-4 slider forward (about halfway) on the hub but not far enough to displace the strut keys. Some sliders are very loose and can drop off the hub. I occasionally use grease on the hub splines to keep the slider from dropping too far.

## 10 Install Reverse Idler and Thrust Washer

Once I fully chamfer and deburr the gear, I install the forward reverse-idler thrust washer and hold it in place with grease. The next step is to drop in the reverse idler. Make sure the backside of the teeth faces the thrust washer. Be sure to pay attention to the position of the countershaft.

## 12 Install Gasket on Midplate

*Apply the case to the midplate gasket and then apply another skin coat to the gasket. Use this method on* every gasket surface on the transmission. Never use silicone sealant because it takes days to dry. Once clamped, the 51813 Permatex sets up within 15 minutes.

## 13 Position 3-4 Slider on Mainshaft

## 14 Install Mainshaft in Case

Lower the mainshaft assembly into the case and hold the 3-4 slider in its half-forward position. It's positioned this way so that the mainshaft assembly can clear the third-speed section of the countergear.

## 16 Install Washer on Rear Idler

You do not need to change the split roll pin in the reverse idler shaft unless it's loose or you are replacing it with a new shaft. Place the .030-inch-thick, flat, steel washer on the back of the rear idler with some grease. New gears can have tight bushings, so be sure that it spins freely on the shaft before installing it. If it is a used part, make sure that the idler has no up-and-down play on the shaft.

**BONUS CONTENT**

**How to Disassemble a Muncie 4-Speed Mainshaft (Housing Repair)**

Scan this QR code with your smartphone to view a video that shows the author's technique for a quick disassembly of a mainshaft

## 15 Properly Engage Mainshaft

Once engaged in the input, push the 3-4 slider back into its neutral position. Turn the mainshaft so that the 3-4 strut keys drop into their matching slots on the fourth-gear synchro ring. Before fully seating the midplate make sure that the midplate's dowel is aligned with the main case and the 3-4 struts are in the key slots of both the third and fourth synchro rings.

## 17 Install Idler Shaft in Case

Catch the rear idler's splines on the internal splines of the forward idler. Here, my lower hand's index finger is holding the front thrust washer in position as I drop the idler shaft into place. Install the midplate-to-tailhousing gasket.

## Final Assembly

### 1 Position Reverse Shifter Shaft

*Position the reverse shifter shaft forward so it is in "reverse." Use grease to place the reverse-gear fork in the lever arm.*

### 2 Install Tailhousing on Midplate

*Placing it forward makes it easy to attach the fork to the reverse gear. Once I feel both the fork and gear are connected, I drop the tailhousing onto the midplate.*

### 3 Seat Reverse Shifter Shaft

*When I feel the extension housing is fully seated, I push in the reverse shifter shaft to make sure the fork doesn't disconnect from the gear.*

### 4 Tighten Tailhousing Bolts

*Install the tailhousing bolts. I like to use lock washers even though the factory never used them. Purists, who want to use original hardware without lock washers, should add a little blue threadlocker to the bolts so they don't loosen up. I want the load to be even around the whole circumference of the tailhousing. Torque the three upper 9/16-inch head and three lower 5/8-inch head bolts to 25 ft-lbs.*

## 5 Test Output Shaft Operation

*Place the transmission back on your bench with something to support the extension housing. Here, I'm using a block of wood. Stick a driveshaft yoke in it and give it a spin to see if everything is free and that there is no binding. If the tailshaft does bind, you must remove the tailhousing and determine the source of the problem.*

## 6 Install Reverse Shifter Shaft Pin

*Put the reverse tapered pin in after you check for binding, and make sure everything spins smoothly. If you have to pull it apart again, it is one less step to perform. Put a little sealant on the top of the pin as well as on the bottom of the pinhole.*

## 7 Position Gears for Mainshaft Nut Installation

*Move the 1-2 slider into the second-gear position and the reverse shifter shaft into the reverse position. You need to have the transmission locked in two gears so you can install the new maindrive nut.*

## 8 Tighten Mainshaft Nut

*Position the nut with the tapered side facing forward. I use a special heavy-duty wrench for this. (Cheap light-duty wrenches are good for only one or two uses.) Seat the nut with a swift strike from a hammer on the wrench. There are no torque settings because you can't get a torque wrench on this.*

## 9 Apply Threadlocker and Stake Mainshaft Nut

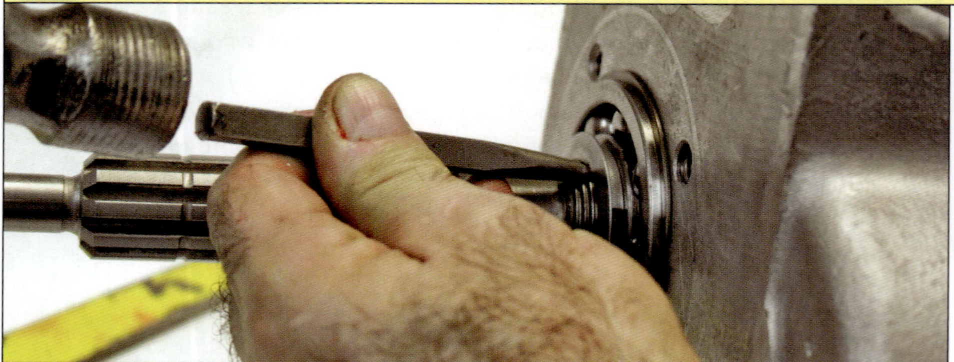

*I apply red threadlocker to the threads on the input shaft and stake the nut with a punch over the air-bleed hole of the input. Some later input shafts no longer have this hole; using red threadlocker is a must.*

## 10 Install Retainer Gaskets

*Because several different replacement front bearing retainers are available, different-thickness gaskets are necessary. Some sets have two .015-inch gaskets that can be stacked. Some have one that is .015-inch and the other is .030-inch thick. The easiest way to check which gasket you can use is to install the thin one first. Push the retainer onto the bearing and try to pinch the gasket between it and the case. Try to pull the gasket out. If you can't, use that gasket. If you can, install the thicker one.*

## 11 Install Bolts and Lock Plates

*I pre-position the bolts in the lock plates and apply sealant to them. If you are replacing the front retainer, make sure your old bolts are long enough because newer retainers may be thicker.*

## 12 Torque Front Retainer Bolts

*Use a 9/16 socket and torque the four bolts to 25 ft-lbs. Once the retainer is installed, clean up excess sealant and bend the lock tabs over.*

## 13 Position Internals for Sidecover Installation

*Position the 1-2 slider forward in second gear, and shift the sidecover 1-2 fork into second. You need to be in second gear to clear the reverse idler case boss.*

## 14 Install Sidecover

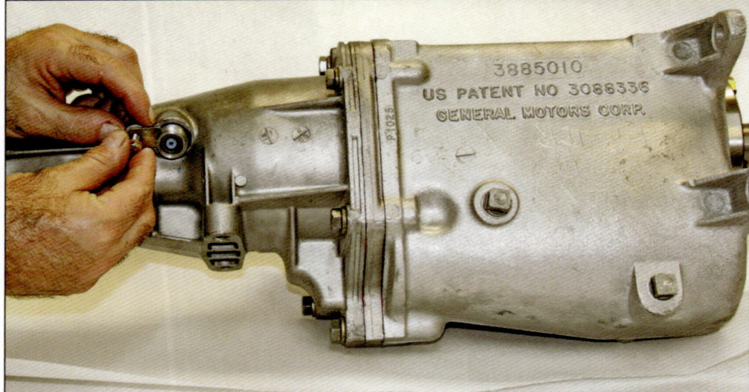

The sealant on the cover gaskets also acts as a thread-locker. Tilt the top of the cover down and catch the upper parts of both shift forks in their respective sliders first, then lower the cover into place.

## 15 Torque Sidecover Bolts

Use a 1/2-inch socket and torque the 7 sidecover bolts to 18 ft-lbs. Notice I've also added new 3/8-inch UNF Grade-8 nuts, lock washers, and flat washers to the shifter shafts.

## 16 Install Speedometer Gear

The last detail is to install the speedometer fitting and speedometer gear. (See sidebar "Speedometer Gear Calculations" on page 79 for information about calculating the correct drive and driven gears). Place the fitting hold into the groove of the fitting. Use a 7/16-inch socket and torque the bolt and lock washer to 10 ft-lbs. Notice the new fill and drain plugs on the main case.

**BONUS CONTENT**

Muncie 4-Speed Rebuilding Upgrades

Scan this QR code with your smartphone to view a video that shows Muncie 4-speed rebuild upgrade tips.

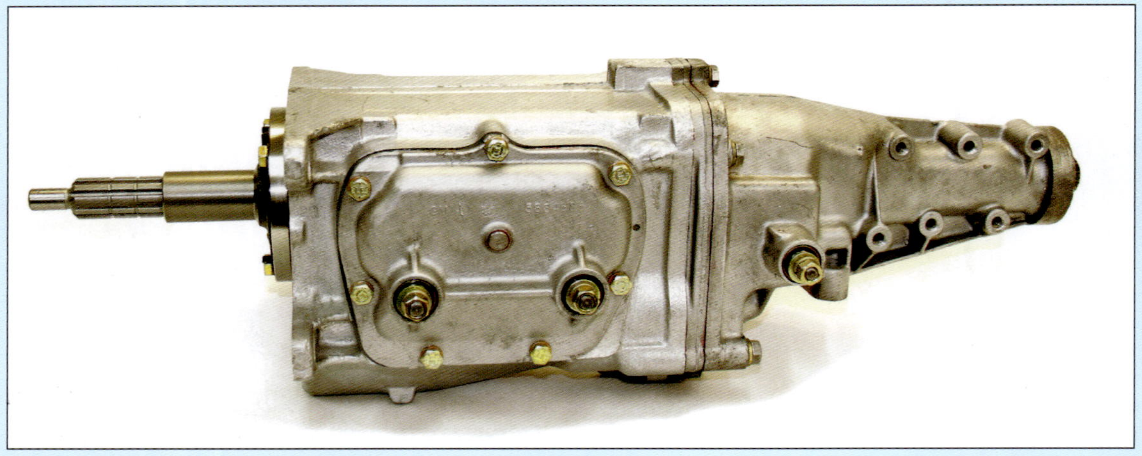

Here is the result of our rebuild. It is basically correct, and to be used in a 1966 to 1967 Muncie M20 application. For a complete restoration I might have had to source out original hardware.

# HIGH-PERFORMANCE MUNCIES

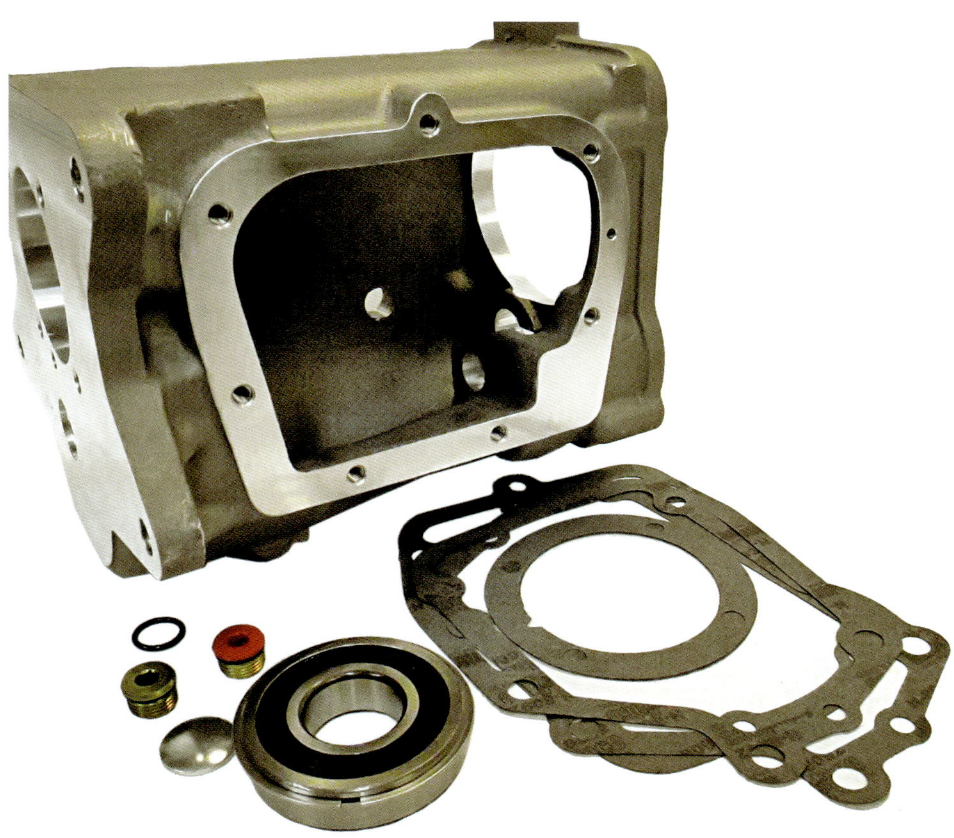

*This heavy new Auto Gear SuperCase comes complete with a wider bearing, gaskets, soft plug, and fill and drain plugs.*

The OEM Muncie 4-speed was aging, few clean used gearboxes were available, the demand for Muncie gearboxes was growing, and the aftermarket had an opportunity to make the Muncie better. A new Muncie gearbox would provide a solid foundation for high-performance and racing applications. All of these factors led to a creation of a new breed of Muncie gearbox. In 1999 I was getting frustrated with the lack of good Muncie cases. Apparently I was not the only one.

## Auto Gear Equipment

George Sollish, president of Auto Gear Equipment (AGE) decided to do something about it. George's grandfather, Irving Sollish, founded Auto Gear and it had been in the manual transmission parts business since 1945. Its mission then was "to provide drivetrain rebuilders with affordable access to the highest quality OEM replacement parts." Today the company designs and manufactures specialized transmissions for off-highway vehicles as diverse as golf course utility vehicles, rough-terrain lift trucks, and street sweepers, as well as a complete line of Muncie

4-speed replacement parts. They actually manufacture every part needed to build a completely new Muncie transmission.

Because they sold parts for drive-train rebuilders, I often purchased original-equipment Muncie ACDelco parts from AGE. They were also a top warehouse distributor for Zoom (Perfection Hy-Test), New Process, and BorgWarner parts. I started dealing with them in 1981. George could see the demand for Muncie parts was growing.

Other manufacturers seemed less and less interested in stocking anything related to Muncies. This is a common disease. Big companies don't operate on the scale of small industries, and as a result, they discontinue parts once production vehicles stop using them. They fail to look at the life-span production numbers.

I remember getting a call from George in 1999. He was talking about a new case design; he had some great ideas and was willing to hear ideas from others as well. Unlike other companies that design products for manual transmissions, Auto Gear took the time to speak to rebuilders and ask them for a "wish list." It makes sense because we are the people who work on these transmissions and have first-hand knowledge of any reoccurring issues.

For example, I have seen many companies fail at releasing a new 5-speed design because the transmission was designed by someone who never owned a muscle car or did not have first-hand knowledge about how the transmission would be used.

### The SuperCase

In the fall of 2000, the Super-Case went into production and the high-performance Muncie transmissions took a big leap forward. The

*The Auto Gear production floor is filled with new Muncie main case and extension housing castings. AGE is a leader in manufacturing new Muncie parts and complete transmission assemblies cast and machined in the United States.*

*George Sollish is holding a freshly machined Muncie SuperCase. More than 5,000 new cases have been sold since they were put into production in 2000. These castings are much stronger than the originals. They use a wider sealed front bearing and have thicker mounting ears.*

base casting design is far superior and much stronger than the OEM case. Cast out of 356 T6 aluminum alloy, it has fewer production cores, which means fewer parting lines in the casting. This case features thicker and more uniform walls. The mounting ears have added material for additional reinforcement.

More material at the front of the case supports a stronger full-width 6307N bearing. This standard-size bearing can be ordered as a sealed bearing to reduce bearing particle contamination and front oil leakage. Both front and rear bearings are now standard sizes, so you can easily order high-quality replacements. The added material in the front allows for soft-plug sealing of the countershaft. The case uses Zero-Leak Gold fill and magnetic drain plugs. This is a major improvement from the old-style 1/2-inch NPT plugs, which can stretch the case when overtightened and frequently seize or leak.

Along with the improvements, George made sure the design still looked like a Muncie case.

*This new case was installed on an M20 Muncie. You can see how the soft plug sealing of the countershaft works. I like to use a steel plug and replace the aluminum plug supplied by Auto Gear.*

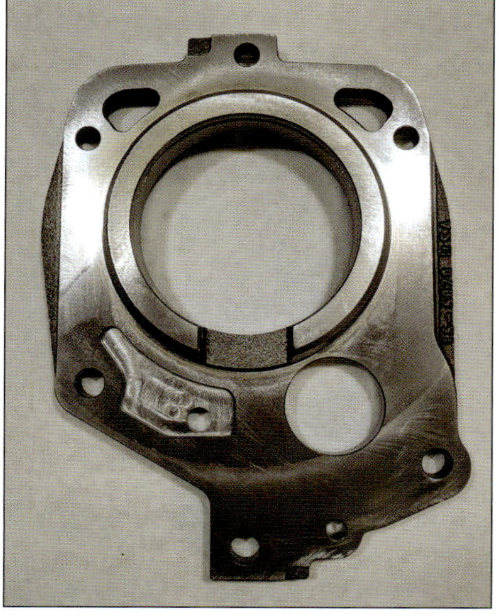

*The factory aluminum plate had a sloppy bearing fit. The slide-hammer effect of a heavy mainshaft tends to elongate the rear bearing snap ring groove which creates excessive gear train endplay. The new nodular iron plate designed by Paul Cangialosi has a tighter rear bearing fit, is flat within .0005 inches, acts as a main case girdle and anchors the lower countershaft to it.*

### Repair Parts Compatibility

A few months after the initial release of the SuperCase, I spoke to George about manufacturing iron midplates, and after that meeting, AGE planned to make new midplates, tailhousings, and sidecovers. The goal was to make all the parts backward compatible, so the rebuilder could repair old transmissions.

On the business side, it allowed the company to fund future endeavors with sales from parts. This worked quite well. Over a five-year period, Auto Gear and a small group of authorized dealers were able to build completely new transmissions.

With this approach, people can build Auto Gear units with a mix of used, new, or inferior parts. You need to carefully select the source of the transmission. If an AGE SuperCase is filled with substandard parts, you can bet its service life will be shorter and it will fail under extreme use.

You need to buy a Muncie transmission from a reputable dealer or manufacturer so you know that you are purchasing an actual new transmission. It's quite common to see "Auto Gear M22" transmissions listed on eBay with Chinese gears and used sidecovers. When Auto Gear or a reputable shop assembles a new Muncie with new parts, you get experienced builders assembling new gearboxes, you get realistic feedback, and more transmissions are brought into the marketplace.

## High-Performance Gearsets

When all major case components became available, it was time to start re-engineering the gearset design. The M22 platform was the foundation for a new series of ratios. To meet the demands of different driving applications several new ratios were offered along with the standard M22 ratio.

The M22/M21 was the standard close ratio offered by General Motors. The M22X is an extra-close ratio for those needing a tighter drop in RPM between third and fourth. The M22 and M22X are used primarily in road racing today.

Although some people running old-school setups with 4.56:1 rear gearing still prefer the M22, most prefer the

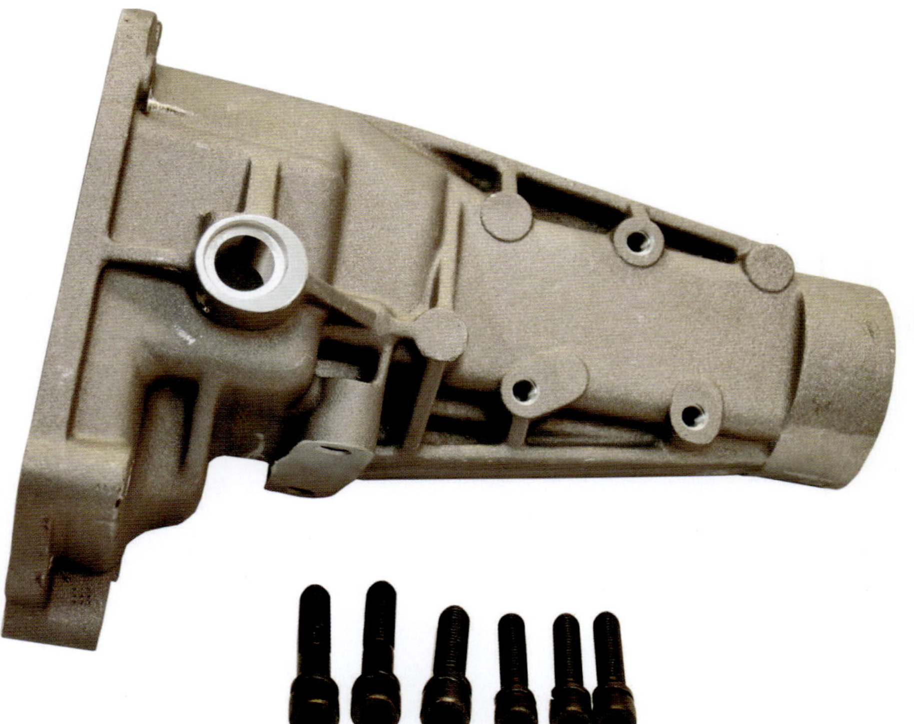

*The new Auto Gear sidecover was designed to address the problem of elongated shifter shaft bores. It comes complete with detents, shifter shafts, spring, and seals. The bores have replaceable standard-size Oilite bushings.*

*The tailhousing has been improved with an upper backbone rib to make it more rigid. It also comes with a 1/4-inch pipe fitting for those wishing to use air vents. The rear bushing is reamed to size in production, assuring bushing concentricity within the tail's centerline. The reverse shifter shaft boss was also reinforced. It comes with new hardware if you order it separately. I have used hundreds of these with no breakage issues or bushing problems.*

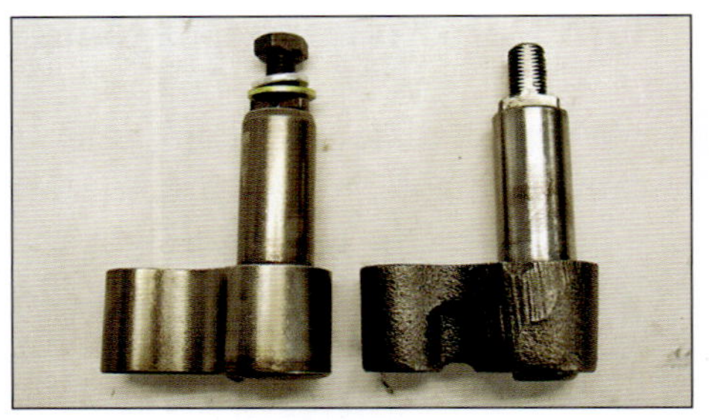

*An old-style arm (right) often cracked where the flat portion of the shaft drives the arm. The billet steel arm (left) is a huge improvement. An adapter clip is supplied when replacing later bolt on–style shafts. Because these shafts are .001-inch oversize from the factory shafts, you can ream out older covers to accept them and restore elongated bores.*

*All new sidecovers come with universal shifter shafts. The new shaft design (left) is hardened and TIG welded to the lever arm. The standard stud-type shaft (right) is replaced by this design. It uses a Grade-8 5/16-24 threaded bolt instead of a stud.*

*The hardened-steel shifter shafts always side-load the soft aluminum cover bores. This causes oil leaks and lost shifter motion. Originally, the design used needle rollers in the bore; it was later changed to full-length Oilite bushings for added support.*

M22W for street use. The M22W has the perfect ratio to split the difference between the standard close and wide ratios. The 3-4 drop is only 4 percent more than that of the M22, but it is 6 percent less than the standard M20.

The M22Z addresses the issue of people wanting economy but not necessarily wanting to go to a 5-speed. It is the widest-ratio 4-speed. You can drop your rear axle ratio to 3.08:1 and use an M22Z with good results. I would not recommend it for serious street/drag racing because of the ratio spreads. Nevertheless, when compared to the M20, it's a good

## M22 Ratio Comparison Chart

| | First-Gear Ratio | % RPM Drop | Second-Gear Ratio | % RPM Drop | Third-Gear Ratio | % RPM Drop | Fourth-Gear Ratio |
|---|---|---|---|---|---|---|---|
| M22 | 2.199 | 25 | 1.640 | 22 | 1.274 | 22 | 1.000 |
| M22X | 2.199 | 32 | 1.506 | 22 | 1.174 | 15 | 1.000 |
| M22W | 2.559 | 31 | 1.752 | 22 | 1.366 | 26 | 1.000 |
| M22Z | 2.984 | 31 | 2.043 | 28 | 1.463 | 32 | 1.000 |
| M20 (for comparison) | 2.520 | 25 | 1.880 | 22 | 1.460 | 32 | 1.000 |

## TKO and M22Z Ratio Comparison Chart

| | First-Gear Ratio | % RPM Drop | Second-Gear Ratio | % RPM Drop | Third-Gear Ratio | % RPM Drop | Fourth-Gear Ratio | % RPM Drop | Fifth Gear Ratio |
|---|---|---|---|---|---|---|---|---|---|
| TKO-600 | 2.87 | 34 | 1.89 | 32 | 1.28 | 22 | 1.00 | 18 | .82 |
| TKO-500 | 3.27 | 39 | 1.98 | 32 | 1.34 | 25 | 1.00 | 32 | .68 |
| M22Z | 2.984 | 31 | 2.04 | 28 | 1.46 | 32 | 1.00 | – | – |

choice and much stronger because of the M22-style gears.

The Tremec TKO is currently the most popular transmission used in 5-speed conversions. The TKO-600 is the closest-ratio 5-speed offered today. The TKO-500 is also very popular, and it is Tremec's wide-ratio option.

The point here is that some 5-speeds are essentially wide-ratio 4-speeds with an overdrive. In fifth gear, a 3.73:1 rear axle with a close-ratio TKO-600 would be equivalent to dropping down to a 3.06:1 rear (.81 x 3.73). You can achieve the same economy by changing your rear-end gear to a 3.08:1 ratio, using existing linkages, and simply swapping out your stock M20 gearset to an M22Z without doing any cutting.

### Manufacturing Quality

With every new design that went into production George at Auto Gear used to tell me that he was going to "move the goal posts" and make significant improvements. I must say he has never failed. Placing the caged

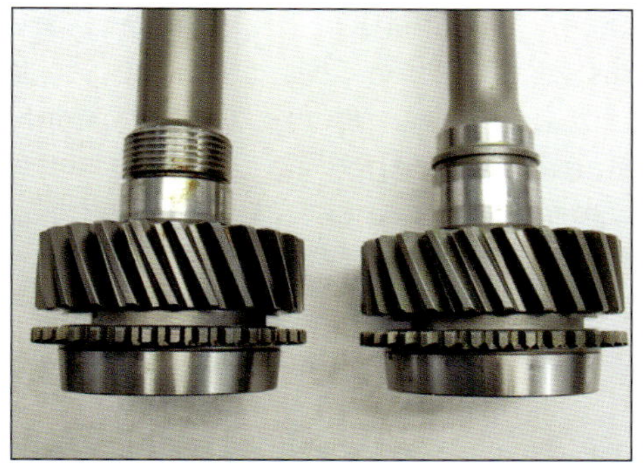

*All M22 gearsets are offered with both 10- and 26-spline inputs for replacement in stock cases. The right input uses a sealed bearing retainer and wider sealed bearing. It is retained by a snap ring while the one on the left is retained by a gland nut. These should only be used with a SuperCase.*

*If you have a new input shaft with a front seal, you must use a matching front-bearing retainer that accepts it. The standard retainer on the left is machined for the old-style gland nut and the right retainer accepts a seal. The seal part number was the same one used in every T5, Super T10, and Saginaw transmission to ensure availability from any parts store.*

*Countershaft support is critical in keeping a gearset from exploding. The new countershafts have a 3/8-16 NC thread that allow them to be fastened to the iron midplate.*

*For stronger gears to be a benefit, the countershaft must be supported better. A large steel thrust button now supports the front of the countershaft and the rear of the countershaft is fastened to the iron midplate.*

*The bolt holding the countershaft to the rear iron midplate is torqued to 35 ft-lbs. This aids in keeping the shaft from walking forward and adds extra support. The front steel thrust button spreads the downward load over a larger diameter (1½ versus .992 inch) reducing front-hole elongation and eliminating leaks.*

needles inside the input shaft has always been a problem because of the sharp internal lip and transition. Because all the others basically copy what General Motors did, all aftermarket input shafts have this annoying feature.

*Both 27- and 32-spline mainshafts are rifle-drilled to reduce rotating mass. More than 1 pound of material is removed in this process. Another great advantage is shaft cooling. Oil can now dissipate heat more quickly under rotating gears.*

The Auto Gear inputs have a tapered transition that allows for faster assembly. This is a basic problem that most people do not understand when they are dealing with aftermarket gears. I know this from first-hand experience; and, more important, this is a problem with the automotive aftermarket in general.

Gears made in China and India are reverse engineered. The original part is simply shipped overseas to a company, and the personnel are asked to make a copy. Typically, the client, who is contracting the run of these copies, doesn't create a three-dimensional model or drawing. As a result, these gears are not made within tolerances or material specifications. The part has been manufactured, it looks good, and it's shipped to the United States for sale. However, something has been lost in translation and in reality it's actually a weak copy of the original.

Unfortunately, the client has no way to check what this "traditional loss" is until the gears are sold. These gears are typically noisy or explode. You need to only select the highest quality, and you need to select the gears from a reputable seller. Some sellers have been dishonest about the origin of these inferior gears and have claimed that the gears were made in the United States. Any eBay sellers claiming these gears are made domestically are lying. In fact, only Muncie speedometer gears are made in the United States. In other words, don't opt for or settle for inexpensive gears of dubious manufacturing quality.

AGE deals with manufacturers who study the drawings and have the means to measure, inspect, and make sure that the final product actually matches the specifications. That is a huge advantage in avoiding costly mistakes and assuring product quality. Currently, AGE manufactures all parts for the Muncie in the United States except for the front bearing, thrust washers, and gears. Those gears are all made in Italy according to AGE prints and specs.

## Muncie Design Features

Let's take a look at some of the new component designs and how I have incorporated them into several new product designs. I primarily build four lines of Muncies: street drivers, drag specials, road/endurance racers, and 4x4 off-road vehicles. New AGE products allow me to continue to offer improvements to these markets.

The AGE M23 program once again moved the "goal posts." The first-gear tooth pressure angle was changed to 20 degrees, which made for a wider tooth profile. The normal older first-gear tooth combination of 17/36 was changed to 16/34. Having fewer teeth within the same diameter creates stronger teeth.

The countergears were designed to be modular and that allows the end user to mix and match gearsets with two basic stub shafts. The addition of the thrust-button case added additional support to the front countershaft.

I use the M23 components to make my "Drag Special" Muncies. By using the modular design I can create a 4-speed transmission with a 2.56:1 first, 1.88:1 second, 1.37:1 third, and 1.00:1 fourth. These ratios add a 27-percent drop in RPM with every gear change.

*The new "Uni-Cluster" countergear needs no spacer tube. It's offered in M20, M22, and M22W ratios. The spacer section is machined into the internal bore. Eliminating the split spacer tube makes the needles easier to load and cuts down on needle skewing because the spacer no longer rocks in the bore. This is the best standard OEM replacement gear available today.*

*This is a complete AGE modular M23 gearset. This is what I use to build my Drag Special 4-speed. It has a 9310–nickel alloy modular stub shaft and sealed front input shaft. The tapered design of the input acts as a torsion bar, absorbing shock loads. I have never had this input shaft break, even when the Muncie is mated to an 800-hp engine. This is fitted in a thrust-button case.*

*First-gear sleeves have dynamic oiling, which offers added oiling as well as support. These components are the basis for building standard-duty M22-series transmissions as well as great upgrades for older Muncies.*

*The inside of a thrust-button case looks like this. The specially heat-treated and coated button increases the load-bearing surface of the countershaft, acts as a front thrust washer, and seals the front.*

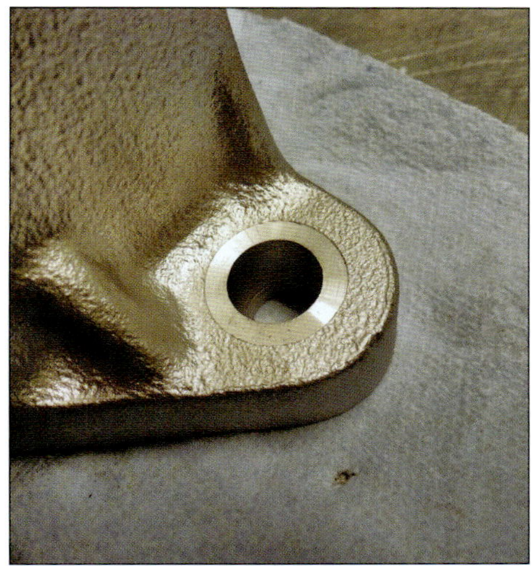

*Every performance unit gets the mounting ears spot faced to ensure a flat surface for mounting bolts and lock washers.*

The SuperCase on the left has been machined for a thrust button while the SuperCase on the right is the standard version, which accepts a soft plug to seal the countershaft. You can see that the left case has a sizable increase in load-bearing area because of the thrust button.

Case venting is often overlooked, but you need to consider it. You don't want pressure levels in the case to rise too high. Most street transmissions use a standard air vent with a 3/8-inch hole. As pressure levels rise from heat and the internal pumping motion of fluids, oil can blow out the transmission. The latest revision of the iron midplate allows for both the forward main case cavity and extension housing internal pressures to easily be equalized by drilling two 3/8-inch holes. Oil can block the passage of air, so having the case compartments equalize above the oil level prevents oil from blowing out vent caps.

The left gear is the standard 36-tooth first gear. Compare it to the newer-design 34-tooth gear on the right. It's easy to see how much wider the teeth are.

The stub shafts come as a first- and second-gear pair. The actual third and maindrive section are pressed-on and held in place with huge retaining rings.

The increased pressure angle of the 34-tooth gear (right) yields more torque capacity, but it increases noise levels. The added expense of a 34-tooth system may pay off with less breakage.

I have never had any of the rings fail. The new countergear components and stub shaft teeth are no longer hobbed; they are ground for better finish after heat-treating to improve profile accuracy. I modified some large pliers to install the rings because I was not happy with the standard "Tru-Arc" pliers available.

*A 16-tooth first-gear section shaft is shown on the left, so you can get an idea of how fewer teeth within the same diameter can yield additional strength. The one on the right has 17 teeth.*

*These are two assembled modular countergears. The beauty of this design is than you can change ratios to create sets that work better for your specific application. Notice the different maindrive sections.*

*This complete Spec-25 gearset is ready for installation. The Spec-25 is a road-racing transmission I designed to be legal in historic Trans-Am racing classes or any other class requiring a synchronized 4-speed. The gears are hand deburred if needed, shot-peened, and finally surface enhanced.*

*This first-gear comparison shows that the surface enhancement extends into the valley between the teeth. Other inferior methods tend to miss this and can actually weaken the part.*

## Road Racing and Endurance Use

When building a transmission for endurance use, heat and shock loads are a main concern. I build the Spec-25 Muncie to fill a need in certain racing classes, such as the historic Trans-Am series, which requires factory-synchronized 4-speeds. In addition, the "Spec-25" name commemorates 25 years in business at the time of its introduction.

Several companies super-finish gears for improved performance, lon-gevity, and heat management. REM Surface Engineering uses Isotropic Superfinish to treat the surface of its Muncie gears. With this process, the gear-tooth surface is enhanced so the surface is as smooth as glass and looks like a mirror. Refining the surfaces of a transmission's gear teeth to achieve the Isotropic Superfinish means that the gears require no break-in period and produce a cooler gearbox opera-tional temperature. In addition, gear-tooth wear, pitting, and spalling are greatly reduced; rotational torque is also decreased.

Another way to stress-relieve gears is with shot-peening. Gears are blasted with tiny steel shot to create miniscule dimples in the gear sur-face. Because most fatigue failures originate at the surface, compress-ing the surface with steel shot can

*Another Spec-25 gearset has an additional Tribobond coating from Ionbond, which reduces gear scuffing under extreme loads. This coating has been used in transmissions I built for six-hour endurance races or the seven-day La Carrera Panamericana, which spans eight Mexican states over seven days. Note that the modular countergear design allows the lower 2-3 section to press against each other, which allows for a wider profile to add gusseting strength.*

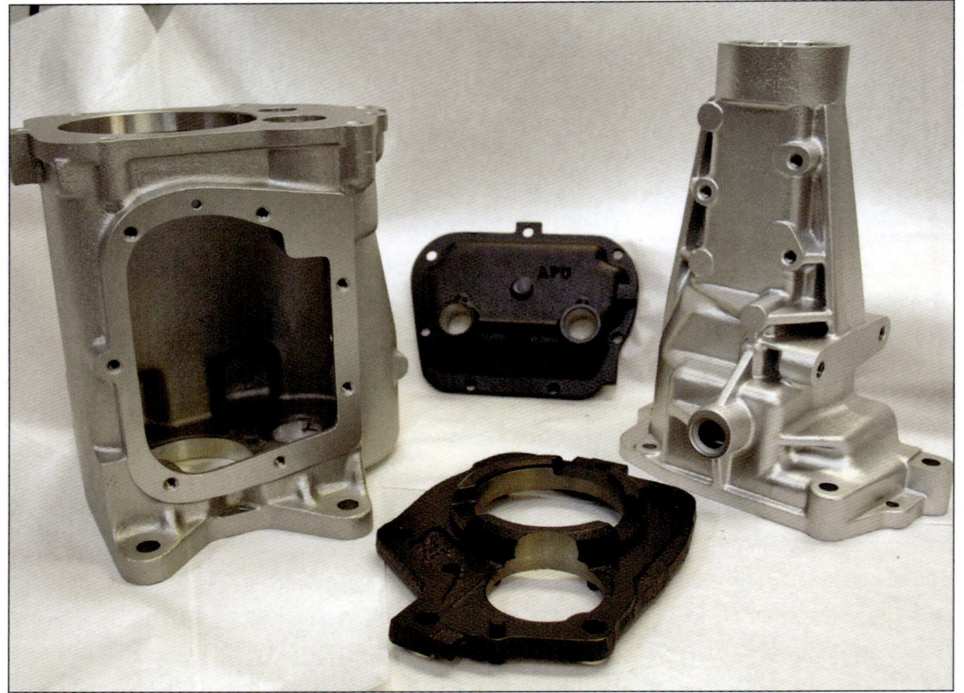

*The SPEC-25 case components are initially deburred by hand to remove any major casting flash and then coated with an anti-stick heat-dissipation coating. You can actually get these coatings in different colors.*

*This assembled sidecover has been coated with a CT non-stick coating, has TIG welded shifter shafts and deburred shift forks with drilled oil dimples.*

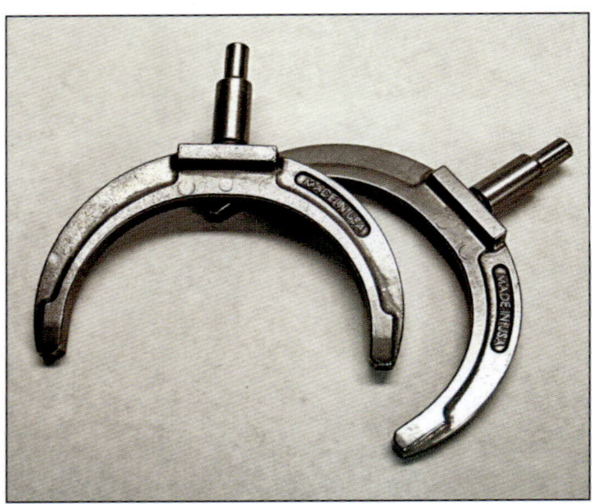

*These are lightweight investment-cast steel forks made by AGE. I sometimes combine these with an 18-tooth synchro assembly to make a very light but strong shift mechanism.*

increase resistance to certain types of fatigue and pitting.

The surface adhesion of gear oil in relation to rotating parts is another factor that should not be overlooked. The oil wants to stick to both the gear and transmission case. This "parasitic friction" creates heat as the oil resists being pulled apart from both surfaces. The Spec-25 cases are treated with a special Teflon-based coating to reduce surface adhesion and promote heat dissipation.

*I install two Oilite bushings in each bore and ream it to fit the shafts with a .751-inch-diameter reamer. This allows the shafts to spin smooth and freely in the bore.*

*The rear midplate also gets a sealed bearing. Any forward motion causes oil to slam into the rear bearing creating pumping losses and internal windage. I recommend the use of sealed or shielded bearings for performance applications. They are much more expensive than conventional bearings and most people have been rebuilding transmission for years with open bearings. However, the reality is that I have never had a bearing fail.*

*When using bearings in road-race transmissions, you want to reduce heat and avoid contamination. I use sealed or shielded bearings in all of my builds. These are* **not** *maximum-capacity bearings. In addition to keeping contaminants out of the bearing, the seals inhibit gear oil turbulence.*

## Bearings

You must use high-quality bearings for a rebuild. If you don't, performance and reliability will suffer. Many manufacturers are making bearings for transmissions today. However, the Muncie's front bearing is an odd size; it was a special bearing made just for that application. At this time, your only choices are Japanese- or Chinese-made versions. Stick to the Koyo, JAF, or NTN brands for this bearing.

The rear bearing is a standard size and is offered by many companies. It is available as a U.S.–made part from SKF. Japanese versions from Koyo, Nachi, and NTN are also acceptable.

## Synchronizers

A transmission built for street use, drag racing, or road racing needs to shift reliably and stay in gear. AGE makes several sizes of synchronizer hubs that allow you to custom-fit sliders to them. The goal is to have a slider and hub combination that has no axial rock so that the slider keeps perfectly parallel as it travels over the hub. If the slider has too much axial rock it can actually vibrate in cars that have harsh drivetrain harmonics, which results in hard shifting. Any excessive motion can allow the slider to deflect under load and come out of gear.

Many people use "torque-locking" sliders to prevent falling out of gear. However, having a slider under load pull itself deeper into gear promotes shift fork wear. It also causes the synchro assembly to overheat and bind under extreme use.

Some applications, such as Pro Shifting, remove the rings completely. Pro-shifted transmissions are often called "crash boxes." When the transmission is Pro Shifted, the 36 engagement teeth of a gear try to mesh with the same number of teeth on the slider. For most stock Muncies,

*Here are some AGE caged needles for the Muncie countergear. It's another trick bearing I use in the SPEC-25 road-race transmission only. These bearings don't generate as much heat as the standard arrangement because the needles are not skewing and rotating against one another. However, I do prefer the standard 112-needle setup for drag-race applications where added support is necessary.*

*This is a roller bearing first-gear assembly (left) that has been shot-peened and surface enhanced. When a transmission is not in first gear, that gear is freewheeling on the mainshaft. If you are in fourth, running at 150 mph, the first-speed gear's rotational speed difference between it and the mainshaft is huge. The heat generated will easily cause the gear to fuse onto a normal first-gear bushing. "Rollerizing" first gear reduces heat, prevents gear-to-shaft seizure, and gets more power to the rear wheels.*

*I use only the best forged synchro rings for Muncies because they are much harder and do not flatten under severe use as cast rings do. I fit each gear individually with a ring that locks on the gear and doesn't rock on the cone. Sometimes rings may have burrs on the threads and it is acceptable to clean them up with a small file.*

this works well below 6,000 rpm and the Muncies can tolerate it. The two components (gear and slider) have a certain relational surface speed between them.

Here's an example to illustrate this operation: You're driving by a picket fence really fast, hanging out of the window, holding a stick, and trying to jam the stick through the pickets. If all the pickets are in place, the gaps are narrow and it's extremely difficult to do (the shift is missed). If you remove every other picket, the gaps between the pickets are larger and it's easier to shove the stick through the pickets (the shift is successful).

If you remove every other tooth on the gear and slider, the surface speed of the two components is cut in half. Therefore, a 36-tooth gear and slider at 7,000 rpm with half of the teeth on each part removed (18 teeth each) will shift as if it were at 3,500 rpm.

## Slick Shifting and Pro Shifting Examples

This input shaft had every other clutch tooth ground off to "slick shift" it. You need to use an 18-tooth slider to make this modification effective. However, the larger window increases backlash between the gear and slider and promotes clutch tooth wear.

You can see how the clutch teeth have worn on this gear as a result of every other tooth being removed. You may gain reduced surface speed that allows a higher RPM shift, but you reduce your holding power by half.

This modified gear has been Pro Shifted. Liberty's Gears actually patented this process years ago. Pro Shifting is not face plating. The gear's 36 clutch teeth are ground off and a 12-lug ring is pressed on and welded into place.

In order to have all 12 splines in contact with the synchro hub, a special hub was made with no strut key slots.

Liberty's 36-tooth slider has been machined down to 12 drive teeth. The huge air gap of the 12-lug system eliminated missed shifts in drag-race applications.

Once I have found a hub that works well with a slider, I mark them as a pair. The left hub is a stock hardened AGE hub. The right hub has had some surface enhancement to remove microscopic burrs.

AGE makes a standard 36-tooth and performance 18-tooth slider. On the Drag Special transmission I keep a 36-tooth on first gear because I want the first-speed gear's 36 clutch teeth fully engaged for maximum support.

The 18-tooth slider is lighter and used on all my SPEC-25 transmissions.

Once I've finished fitting the sliders to the hubs I mark them so I know the exact orientation I need to put them back together.

Once marked, I can take sliders apart to remove the sharp edge that some have in the center. This gives the strut key have a smoother transition and prevents wear when shifting.

Some aftermarket springs have tangs at the end that are too long. This prevents the spring from making direct contact with the strut key, which essentially renders the key useless.

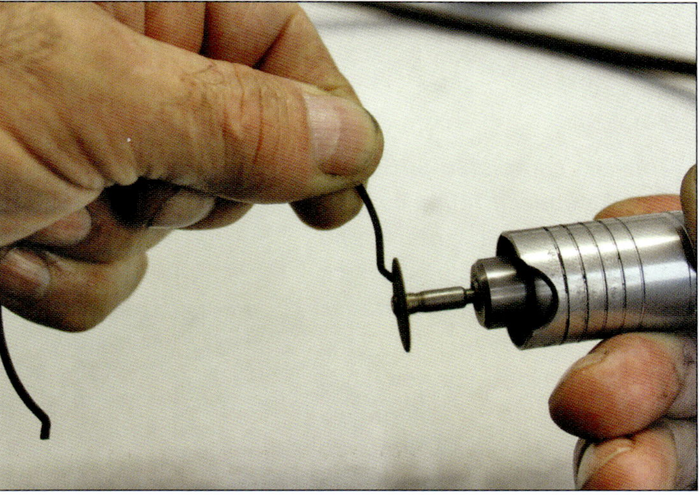

If the tang is too long, such as with this spring, use a rotary tool to remove enough material at the end so that the spring engages the strut key. I grind the tang down a little at a time until the spring makes contact.

*Enough material has been removed from the tang. I can see that it is fully supporting the strut key, which allows the strut to properly function.*

*This is the upper geartrain of the SPEC-25. Notice the shape of the lighter 18-tooth sliders. This particular setup had both sliders and hubs surface enhanced.*

*This completed replacement M22Z Muncie has a 10-spline input and 27-spline output. I built this one for a customer who has a 1967 Corvette with 3.08:1 axle. He wanted to have some fuel economy, yet have great acceleration and the ease of a direct replacement. He was able to use his existing shift linkage and driveshaft.*

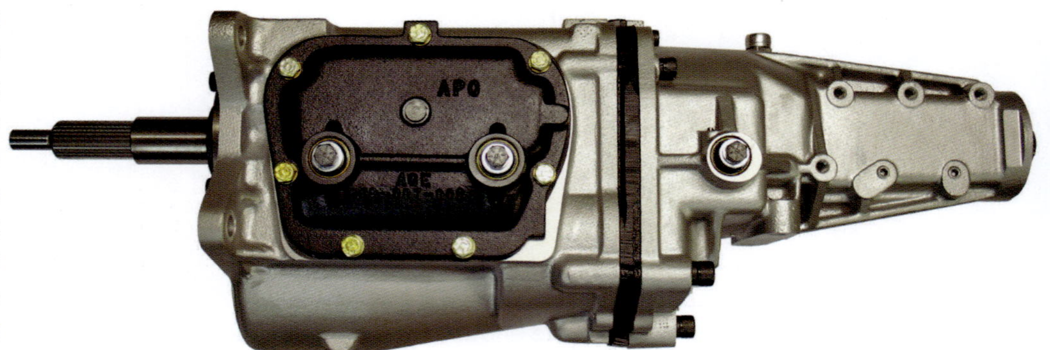

*This is a completed SPEC-25. The special Teflon coating has another advantage. The exterior becomes a non-stick surface, and gasket surfaces clean up very quickly. Plans are in the works for new-style NASCAR synchro assemblies and more ratios, so a SPEC-35 will most definitely be in the future!*

# ADVANCE ADAPTERS 4x4 CONVERSION KIT

*This is a new M22Z 4-speed used in a 4x4 configuration. They have become popular in rock-crawling applications.*

In the early 1970s, the Muncie was readily available. It is a durable, reliable, and efficient 4-speed transmission so it was only a matter of time before someone used it for off-road 4x4 applications. In 1971 John Partridge designed a kit to adapt the Muncie 4-speed to a Jeep Dana 300 transfer case. It became very popular and was the building block that helped start his company Advance Adapters.

The kit became so popular that people wanted a similar conversion for Toyota Land Cruisers. Currently, kits are available to mate the Muncie with 1946–1979 Jeeps, 1980–1986 Jeeps, 1963–1973 Toyota Land Cruisers, GM New Process model 203 and 205 part-time transfer cases, as well as Dana 300 transfer cases. More than 1,000 4x4 conversions have been completed with these kits. As of 2013, Advance Adapters sells more than 1,500 transfer cases per year and employs 45 people.

When I started building new Muncie 4-speeds I asked Mike Partridge (son of John) of Advanced Adapters to include the new M22Z 4x4 Muncie in his huge catalog. I felt that the 2.98:1 first gear of the M22Z would be perfect for slow-speed high-torque rock crawling; overdrives and excess weight aren't needed for this application. For this build, I used the thrust-button AGE case and a complete M22Z modular gearset. The ratios of this transmission are 2.98:1 (first), 2.04:1 (second), 1.46:1 (third), and a direct fourth.

The AGE M22Z transmission and retrofit gearset has also become very popular as a standard replacement 4-speed with cars using a 3.08:1 axle. This gives you the economy of an overdrive and maintains good acceleration as a direct fit replacement without cutting up the floor. You can use the stock shifter so the cost ends up being much cheaper than any 5-speed conversion.

Although I am installing this gearset into a 4x4 application, some of the idiosyncrasies of the M22Z discussed here will help you retrofit stock Muncies. I have learned that installing any adapter-type kit requires a bit of patience. Regardless of who makes the kit, very few fit perfectly. The reason is that with so many aftermarket components being made and no standard dimensions documented, some components need a little "massaging" to fit. Because the basic Muncie mainshaft and countergear assembly format is used, I have only included some of the extras unique to this build.

This kit allows you to install a Muncie 4-speed to a Dana 300 transfer case. It is compatible with the 1946–1979 Jeep Dana 18 and 20 with a 6-spline output shaft. For the Muncie, the Jeep Dana 18/20 is 4-1/2 inches too long. The adapter is made of 356 T-6 heat-treated aluminum alloy and it includes a provision for a rear transmission mount. The kit also features a new mainshaft, hardware, gaskets, seals, and complete instructions.

*These are the components of the Advance Adapters Muncie 4x4 kit. You have an adapter rear housing, custom mainshaft, and output bearing, which allow you to mate a Muncie to a Dana 300 transfer case.*

*This splined section mounts the transfer case's input gear to the Muncie.*

*All the synchronizer and reverse gear splines are identical. The 4x4 shaft (top) is much shorter than the stock 32-spline shaft (bottom).*

The Auto Gear M22Z gearset includes first-, second-, third-speed gears; maindrive; modular countergear; reverse idler; front sealed bearing retainer; seal; and retaining rings.

After checking for dings, all the gears are deburred. Assembly of the countergear starts by mating the lower third-gear section to the first/second stub shaft.

## Mainshaft Assembly

The mainshaft assembly procedure for the M22Z is very similar to the reverse of the disassembly process. The synchro assemblies must be properly matched and assembled before pressing the gears onto the mainshaft. These subassemblies should be ready to go on the mainshaft; it will help to keep you organized.

Never press directly on gear surfaces. The lower gear has an old bearing race against it. This grabs closer to the inside diameter of the gear so you should avoid press-surface contact with the gear teeth.

*Important!*

**1  Install Third-Gear Retaining Ring**

After the lower third gear is in place, you must install the third-gear retaining ring and rear lower maindrive ring. Inspect for metal chips in the ring grooves before installing them.

**2  Press on Lower Maindrive**

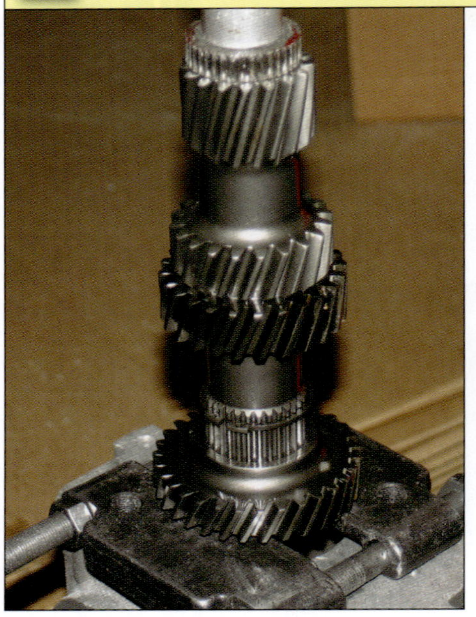

Finally, you need to put the mainshaft in the jig for the arbor press, and press on the lower maindrive section. I spray WD-40 on the splines to prevent them from galling when pressed together.

**3  Install Front Lower Maindrive-Retaining Ring**

Use snap-ring pliers to install the front lower maindrive-retaining ring. The snap ring fits into the channel on the gear. It's a good idea to stagger the ends of the three rings by about 120 degrees. I do this to balance the weight of the rings.

The second and third lower gears can be pressed against each other on the mainshaft; they are much wider than factory gears. As a result, gusseting strength is added.

## Maindrive Inspection

You need to select top-quality maindrive components for your transmission rebuild, and Auto Gear offers a full complement of the best components, including the maindrive. Before you assemble the main drive, make sure that all parts and gears are clean and in good condition.

I found a few dings on the maindrive gear. I'm using a Dremel tool with an abrasive cut-off wheel to smooth the lower gear faces. All gear teeth surfaces should be clean and true. It is not unusual to have dings on new gears.

The M22Z maindrive (left) has a much smaller gear than the standard M22 (right). The 22-tooth count of the M22Z is much less than the 26-tooth standard M22. That is how the lower 2.98:1 first-gear ratio is achieved.

*The Auto Gear maindrives have gone through several design changes. The latest revision moves the engagement teeth and synchro cone in .040 inch. This eliminates having to shim maindrives deeper and improves synchro response.*

*Factory Muncie maindrives had sharp edges, making needle bearings difficult to install. These edges create stress risers and increase metal fatigue.*

*The revised design uses smoother fillets and avoids sharp breaks, making caged needles easy to install and adding strength.*

*New countergears taper the first-gear section toward second gear, which was another revision to avoid sharp edges and improve strength.*

*The countershaft spacer tube has been eliminated. A thicker internal wall offers more rigidity, easier needle assembly, and reduced needle bearing skewing.*

## Gearbox Assembly

The case must be properly conditioned for reassembly. All threads should be cleaned and chased. The counterbore shaft hole has to be within spec and not elongated. If you're using a new AGE SuperCase for your rebuild, you are starting with a strong foundation.

*If you are installing this gearset in an existing Muncie case, you can order it with the old threaded-bearing nut design. Regardless of which style maindrive you use, do not use any additional shims. Compared to the standard M20 maindrive (right), you can see the lower helix angle of the M22Z (left).*

### 1 Install Bearing on Input Shaft

*These gears don't have a very tight bearing press-fit, so you can use a punch to work the bearing down if you don't have access to a press. Using an arbor press places even and consistent force on the bearing, and it is the preferred method for assembly.*

### 2 Install Spacer and Snap Ring

*All the newer 26-spline maindrives use a spacer and retaining ring. The spacer always goes in front of the bearing but behind the ring.*

*The newer-style retaining ring mount with a sealed bearing can only be used if you have the new AGE Super-Case. It allows you to use a front seal, which is necessary during rock crawling because of the steep inclines to which the powertrain is subjected.*

---

**Critical Inspection**

**3 Verify Thread Condition**

*Verify that the threads on any mainshaft are in good condition. Make sure that the nut fastens smoothly on the end of the shaft. This makes it much easier to repair any damaged threads before final assembly.*

**4 Install AGE Bushing on Shaft**

*All new M22-style transmissions use the AGE first-gear bushing. It should always be used with the M22Z gearset, even if you are doing a retrofit, because first gear spins much faster on the mainshaft when in fourth. The bushing promotes improved dynamic oiling.*

---

## 5 Drill Out Midplate Dowel Hole

*The AGE iron midplate uses a standard 5/16-inch dowel. The new extension's dowel hole has to be enlarged to match it.*

*The hole gets extremely close to the edge, so be careful that you don't break through.*

## 6 Remove Dowel for Trial Fitting

*Remove the dowel so that you can trial-fit all of the case parts. You don't want to risk breaking the 4x4 extension.*

## 7 Custom Fit Adapter Housing

*The adapter housing does not fit on the midplate. Indicate the area of concern with a marker pen to see how much material must be removed.*

## 8 Fit Housing

*The fitting process involves filing material off the housing until it fits flush with the midplate.*

## 9 Fabricate Custom Stud

*A stud has to be made because a standard extension-housing bolt doesn't have enough clearance to be installed. Because these castings vary in height, make a stud out of threaded rod that extends 3/4 inch above the surface of the hole.*

## 10 Fit Case Components Together

*Because most of these parts do not fit together well and require filing and grinding it is best to get all the case components fitted with each other correctly. Then you can build the mainshaft assembly and install the countergear and maindrive into the case. (See Chapter 5.)*

## 11 Use AGE Iron Midplate

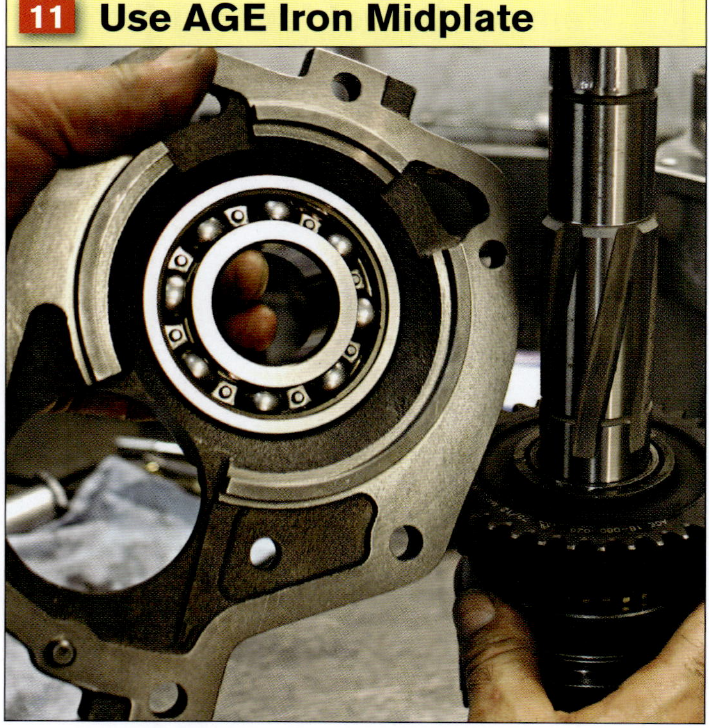

*For added rigidity use an AGE iron midplate on the mainshaft assembly.*

*The completed M22Z 4x4 mainshaft with iron midplate does not use a speedometer gear.*

## 12 | Ream Extension Housing

The 4x4 extension housing needs to be reamed open by .001 inch to accept the later-design AGE heavy-duty shifter shafts.

## 13 | Install Case Air Vent

If you are using a completely sealed system, you need to have a case air vent installed. Drill the case, tap it for a 1/4-inch pipe-thread, and use a baffled, filtered vent.

## 14 Tap Pipe Threads

*Important!*

**!** *When tapping any casting with a pipe thread, use extra care to tap and trial fit your part in small steps. With this case, there is not much material and it is very easy to over-tap the case and lose the sealing action of the pipe thread.*

## 15 Install Reverse Shifter Shaft

*When installing the reverse shifter shaft in this casting, it can slide off the detent on either side because there is nothing preventing it from walking out too far.*

## 16 Install Countergear and Maindrive Shafts

*Use the standard countergear and maindrive case installation procedure but leave out the rear thrust washer to help the cluster gear drop down more; this allows easier maindrive installation. Once in place, reinstall the washer and then the countershaft.*

## 17 Install Front Bearing Retainer on Transmission

*Unlike the standard M22 gearsets, the Z maindrive gear section can fall into the front case bearing bore. You can place the front bearing retainer on the transmission with just two bolts to prevent that from happening.*

## 18 Place Mainshaft in Case

*Even if you are using the standard mainshaft-to-case assembly, leave the reverse gear off the mainshaft.*

## 19 Machine Idler Shaft

*The reverse idler bore is very tight in the 4x4 case. It creates an air lock and does not allow the case to seat. Grind a flat in the idler shaft from the end to the front of the dowel to let air escape.*

## 20 Align Midplate in Case

*Because the midplate has a locating dowel (and I have another threaded rod in the main case), there is no wiggle room. The 4x4 adapter has to drop straight down.*

**Professional Mechanic Tip**

## 21 Insert Reverse Gear onto Rear Case

*By placing the reverse gear in the adapter you have a straight drop onto the mainshaft and can catch both the midplate dowel and threaded stud. Remember, the detent can easily pop out if the shifter shaft is moved too far in either direction.*

## 22 Install Reverse Tapered Pin

*Install the reverse shifter shaft tapered pin using extreme care so the shaft does not come out too far and drop the detent ball into the transmission.*

## 23 Install Adapter Bearing

*The rear adapter bearing fits tightly into this housing. Avoid cocking it and make sure it is completely seated. Once it is seated, install its retaining ring. Some slide in, and others have to be seated with a light hammer.*

## 24 Install Rear Bearing Assembly

*Install the rear seal carefully by tapping it with a hammer. Then slide in the rear bearing retainer assembly until the rear lip of the retainer is flush with the 4x4 housing.*

## 25 Install Gasket and Cover

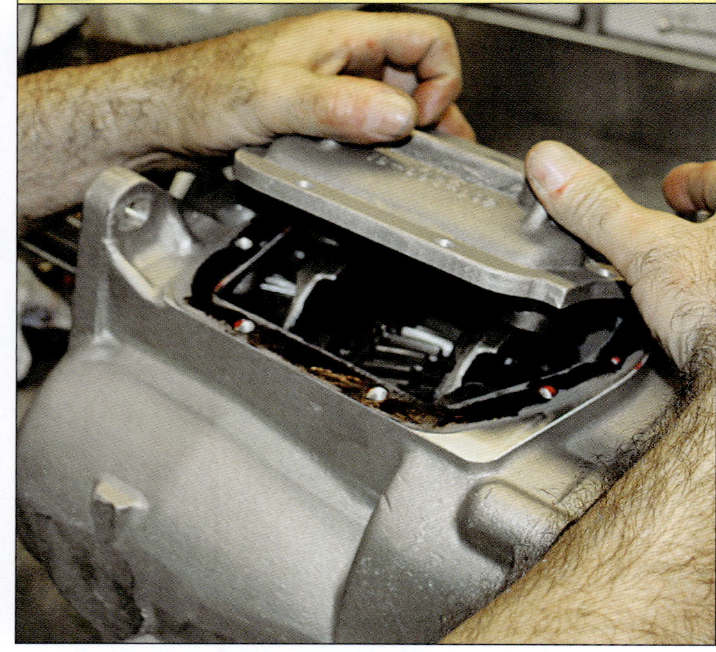

*The AGE cover has universal shifter shafts so you can use any custom shifter. I coat both sides of the gasket with Permatex 51813.*

*The completed M22Z 4x4 transmission has a filtered vent on top of the rear housing.*

*This is a custom Hurst shifter for this application. Advance Adapters sells this complete with a shifter stick and knob that looks like the factory Jeep part.*

*This is a similar conversion that was created for a Toyota Land Cruiser. Notice how far the mainshaft extends from the back of the unit. The shifter for this application mounts on the transfer case.*

# PARTS RESOURCES

I wanted to combine the latest parts with some of the older part numbers in one reference section. It took a great deal of time and research to find original GM part numbers. Although most of these numbers are no longer available, having them as a reference can be valuable for those looking for used parts on the Internet or at automotive swap meets. George Sollish and Eric Malinowski of Auto Gear were extremely helpful with creating three-dimensional illustrations as well as giving me their library of new part numbers.

Aftermarket parts for Muncies are not a new idea. BorgWarner developed a numbering system for manual transmission parts when they began making replacement parts. Each transmission became a numbered series. The Muncie series was No. 297. Other examples are the Ford Toploader (No. 296) and the Chrysler A833 (No. 294). Other companies, such as Perfection Hy-Test (who made the Zoom ring and pinions), also made replacement Muncie gears. Their series number is 312. The main number is then simply followed by another number representing a case, extension housing, speed gear, reverse gear, etc.

BorgWarner has two basic systems. The early system adds a number to the series number: 297-12 is a Muncie first-speed gear. Any variation of that gear will have a letter after the 12. Therefore, 297-12, 297-12A, 297-12B, are all first gears for Muncies but for different applications.

*New gears, such as this brand-new M20 gearset, are machined with closer tolerances than original gears, using better alloys and heat-treatment methods.*

## BorgWarner Suffix Designator

These suffix designators help identify the following components.

| | | | | | | | |
|---|---|---|---|---|---|---|---|
| First gear | 12 | Mainshaft | 2 | Extension housing | 7 | Strut keys | 13 |
| Second gear | 21 | Reverse gear | 36 | Idler gears | 10 | Sidecovers | 148 |
| Third gear | 11 | Idler shaft | 35 | Synchro rings | 14 | Midplates | 107 |
| Maindrive | 16 | Shift fork | 23 | Synchro sliders | 15 | O-rings | 108 |
| Countergear | 8 | Front retainer | 6 | Synchro hubs | 2.5 | | |
| Countershaft | 3 | Main case | 1 | Synchro assemblies | 80 | | |

By 1970 this system has been replaced with a 10-digit system that was in use until the company was sold to Tremec in the 1990s. The first four numbers were the model designator, followed by a 3-digit component part category, followed by a 3-digit unique identifier.

For example, 13-52-085-025 decodes as a T5 5-speed (13-52), a maindrive input (085), and the specific input identification (025). Auto Gear now uses a similar system for the Muncie. The format is the same but is scaled down to an 8-digit system. The Auto Gear system uses a model number. The Muncie is model No. 18, followed by a 3-digit component part category, followed by the unique 3-digit part identifier.

## Component Part Categories

| Number | Part Type | Number | Part Type | Number | Part Type |
|---|---|---|---|---|---|
| 027 | Bearing caps and retainers | 068 | Intermediate shafts (not torque carrying) | 089 | Synchro sleeves |
| 031 | Flanges and yokes | 070 | Gears that are splined or keyed | 090 | Synchro hubs |
| 037 | Shims | | | 091 | Synchro rings |
| 039 | Covers | 077 | Countergears | 096 | Shift forks |
| 065 | Transmission cases | 080 | Gears, free running, first, second, third | 097 | Shift covers |
| 066 | Extension housings | | | 098 | Shift levers |
| 566 | Extension assemblies | 083 | Third gears, free running | 100 | Shift rails |
| 067 | Intermediate shafts | 084 | Idler gears | 127 | Bushings and wear pads |
| 567 | Intermediate shaft assemblies | 584 | Idler gear assemblies | 171 | Mainshafts |
| | | 085 | Input shafts | 671 | Mainshaft assemblies |
| | | | | 410 | Kits |

You will notice in the following chart that when a "5" is placed in front of a category number it becomes an assembly. For example: A front reverse idler for a Muncie is an 18-084-002. The idler is a stand-alone gear. Yet a rear idler is numbered as 18-584-001. The rear idler is an assembly because it comes with bronze bushings installed. I like this system because it is much more detailed than the older system. I hope that now that you have a better understanding of what the numbers actually mean, the catalog makes more sense.

By now you should have a better understanding of how the part number system works. So, with that knowledge, which gear is a 297-11 and which gear is a 297-21?

# Group A: Mainshaft and Extension Housing

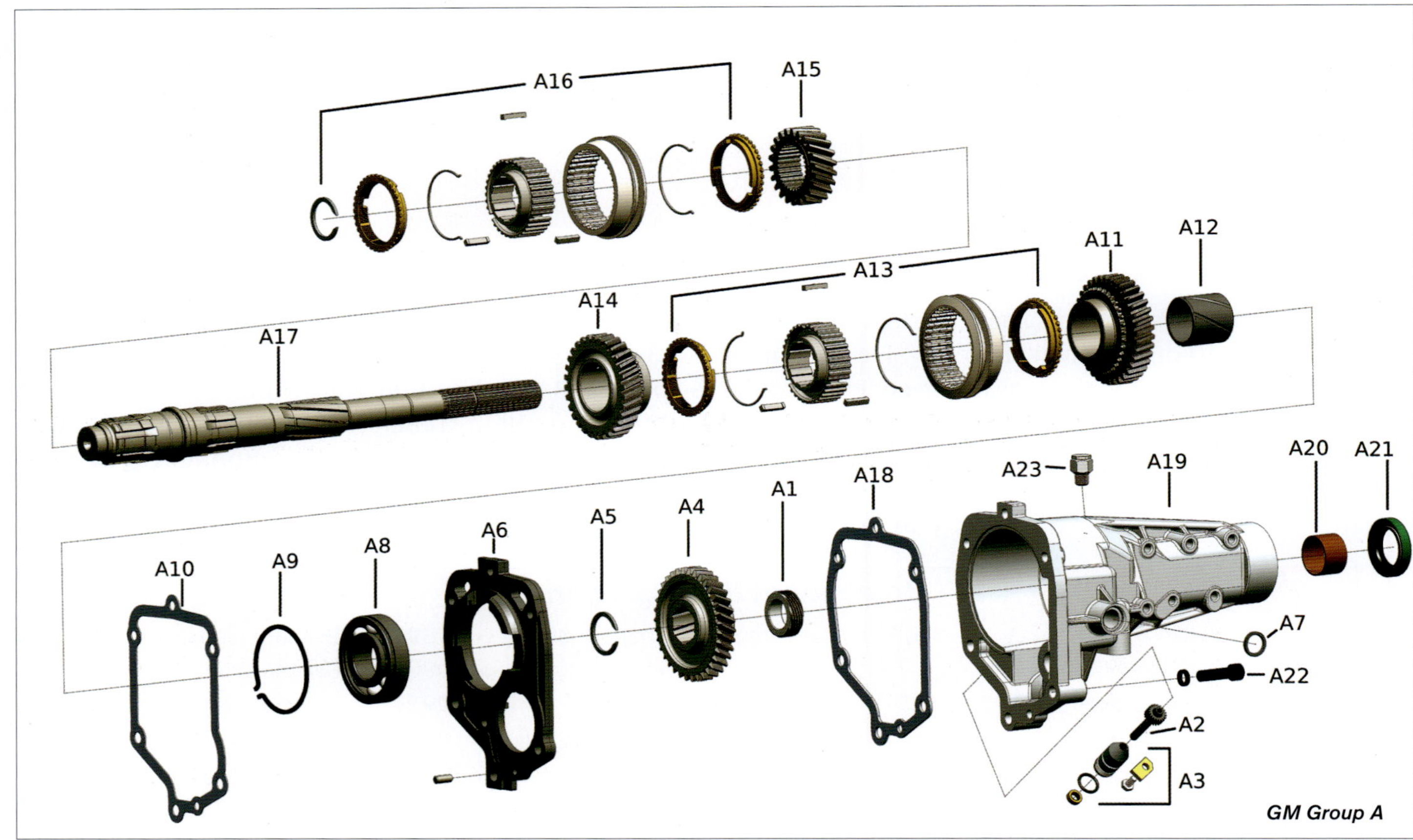


| Group# | Description | Year | OEM# | Replacement # |
|---|---|---|---|---|
| **A1** | **Speedometer Circle Gear** | | | |
| | *These gears have 30-mm bore: used with 27-spline mainshaft:* | | | |
| | L6T steel: 1.92" OD | 1963–1970 | 3845079 | N/A |
| | L7T steel: 1.76" OD | 1963–1970 | 9785023 | N/A |
| | L8T steel: 1.76" OD | 1963–1970 | 3708145 | 3708145 |
| | L7T steel: 1.84" OD | 1963–1970 | | 18-110-006 |
| | L8T steel: 1.84" OD | 1963–1970 | 3708144 | 18-110-007 |
| | L8T nylon 1.84" OD | 1969–1970 | 6261794 | 6261794 |
| | L9T steel: 1.84" OD | 1963–1970 | | 18-110-010 |
| | | | | |
| | *These gears have a 35-mm bore: used with 32-spline mainshaft:* | | | |
| | L7T steel: 1.84" OD | 1971–1974 | | 18-110-008 |
| | L8T steel: 1.84" OD | 1971–1974 | 3978758 | 18-110-009 |
| | L9T steel: 1.84" OD | 1971–1974 | | 18-110-011 |
| | | | | |
| | Speedometer circle-gear retainer clip (used with 8T nylon gear only) | 1969–1970 | 6261781 | 6261781 |
| **A2** | **Speedometer Pencil Gear** | | | |
| | *This gear used with 1.92" OD circle gear:* | | | |
| | L20T steel | | 3860329 | N/A |
| | | | | |
| | *These gears used with 1.76" OD circle gears:* | | | |
| | L22T green nylon | | 3860345 | 3860345 |
| | L23T black nylon | | 3860346 | 3860346 |
| | L24T yellow nylon | | 3860347 | 3860347 |
| | L25T orange nylon | | 3860348 | 3860348 |

| Group# Description | Year | OEM# | Replacement # |
|---|---|---|---|
| *These gears used with 1.84" OD circle gears:* | | | |
| L17T purple nylon | | 3987917 | 3987917 |
| L18T brown nylon | | 3987918 | 3987918 |
| L19T natural nylon | | 3987919 | 3987919 |
| L20T blue nylon | | 3987920 | 3987920 |
| L21T red nylon | | 3987921 | 3987921 |
| L22T grey nylon | | 3987922 | 3987922 |
| **A3**   **Speedometer Adapter Assembly** | | | |
| Bullit fitting with seal and O-ring | | 345215 | 345215 |
| Fitting oil seal | | 3869910 | 3999L |
| Fitting hold-down bracket | | 3708148 | 3708148 |
| Bolt 1/4-20 x 5/8 HHCS | | | 87914719 |
| Fitting O-ring | | 6264903 | 3410L |
| Optional block-off plug | | | 550-014 |
| **A4**   **Mainshaft Reverse Gear** | | | |
| R35: 6-spline upper gear | | 3831748 | WT297-36 |
| Anti-ash circular-spline spring - 2 req'd. | | 3890532 | N/A |
| **A5**   **Mainshaft Rear Bearing Snap Ring** | | | |
| *These snap rings are selective fit:* | | | |
| Snap ring: .070" thick | | 3831755 | 3831755 |
| Snap ring: .085" thick | | 3831756 | 3831756 |
| Snap ring: .095" thick | | 3831757 | 3831757 |
| Snap ring: .100" thick | | 3831758 | 3831758 |
| Snap ring: .105" thick | | 3831759 | 3831759 |
| **A6**   **Mainshaft Rear Bearing Support** | | | |
| Factory aluminum | | 3831752 | N/A |
| Ductile iron (heavy-duty) | | | 18−19672-003 |
| Dowel pin: 5/16" diameter x 1 inch long | | | 06025100 |
| **A7**   **Extension Housing Shaft Seal** | | | |
| Oil seal | | 3831716 | 7410CR |
| **A8**   **Mainshaft Rear Bearing** | | | |
| Open type (SKF 6308NR) | | 907474 | 6308NR |
| Sealed type (Nachi 6308-2NSE9NR) | | | 0-130-020 |
| **A9**   **Mainshaft Bearing Support Snap Ring** | | | |
| All | | 3831749 | 3831749 |
| **A10**   **Mainshaft Bearing Support Gasket** | | | |
| Gasket | 1963–1974 | 3911900 | 18-045-103 |
| **A11**   **Mainshaft 1st Gear** | | | |
| *These are for M20 and M21 transmissions:* | | | |
| Thrust washer | 1963 only | 3831745 | N/A |
| Gear L36T: S36T snap-ring counterbore, used with washer | 1963 only | 3831743 | WT297-12 |
| Gear L36T: S36T used with bushing | 1964–1974 | 3849388 | 18-080-025 |
| Gear L36T: S36T used with roller bearing - road race | 1964–1974 | | 18-080-023 |
| *These are for M22 transmissions:* | | | |
| Gear L36T: S36T used with bushing | 1965–1972 | 3924786 | 18-080-026 |
| Gear L36T: S36T used with roller bearing - road race | | | 18-080-024 |
| *These are for M23 extreme-duty transmissions:* | | | |
| Gear L34T: S36T used with bushing | 1965–1972 | 3924786 | 18-080-027 |
| Gear L34T: S36T used with roller bearing - road race | | | 18-080-028 |
| *These are complete 1st-gear rollerized bearing kits* | | | |
| Kit w/M20/M21 1st-gear and roller bearing assembly | 1964–1974 | | 18-410-032 |
| Kit w/M22 1st-gear and roller bearing assembly | 1965–1972 | 3965752 | 18-410-014 |
| Kit w/M23 1st-gear and roller bearing assembly | | | 18-410-039 |

| Group# Description | Year | OEM# | Replacement # |
|---|---|---|---|
| **A12  Mainshaft 1st-Gear Bushing/Bearing** | | | |
| Plain bushing with oil grooves | 1964–1974 | 3978781 | 18-103-001 |
| Factory M22 bushing w/oil flats use 18-103-001 | 1965–1972 | 3932228 | N/A |
| Roller bearing race | 1965–1972 | 326578 | 18-103-002 |
| Roller bearing | 1965–1972 | 9433516 | 0-132-012 |
| Roller bearing spacer | 1965–1972 | 326579 | 18-053-001 |
| **A13  Mainshaft 1-2 Synchronizer Parts** | | | |
| Snap ring 1-2 synchro hub | 1963 | 3832626 | N/A |
| Synchro ring w/o support shoulder - 2 req'd. | 1963–1965 | 3831733 | WT297-14 |
| Synchro ring w/support shoulder - 2 req'd. | 1966–1974 | 3880850 | WT297-14A |
| Synchro ring w/support shoulder, forged HD - 2 req'd. | 1966–1974 | 344243 | WT297-14D |
| Synchro hub | 1963–1965 | NSS | NSS |
| Synchro hub standard replacement | 1965–1974 | NSS | WT297-2.5A |
| Synchro hub hardened | | | 18-090-002 |
| Synchro hub hardened - oversize | | | 18-090-003 |
| Synchro hub hardened - oversize no key slots | | | 18-090-004 |
| Strut dog - 3 req'd. | | 3915050 | WT297–1977 |
| Strut spring - 2 req'd., thin | 1963 | 591914 | N/A |
| Strut spring - 2 req'd., medium | 1964–1965 | 3853805 | N/A |
| Strut spring - 2 req'd., wide | 1966–1974 | 3920775 | N/A |
| Strut spring - 2 req'd., modern replacement | 1963–1974 | | 4682AJ |
| Sliding clutch, 36-spline | 1963–1974 | NSS | T85B-15 |
| Sliding clutch, 36-spline, "torque-locking" | | | T85B-15A |
| Sliding clutch, 18-spline, "slick shift lightened" | | | 18-089-001 |
| 1-2 synchronizer assembly | 1963–1974 | 357238 | 18-590-011 |
| 1-2 synchronizer assembly, "torque-locking" | 1963–1974 | 344241 | 18-590-013 |
| **A14  Mainshaft 2nd Gear** | | | |
| Gear L30-s36T: M20/M21 | 1963–1974 | 357226 | 18-080-018 |
| Gear L30-s36T: M22 | 1965–1972 | 3879999 | 18-080-019 |
| Gear L29-s36T: M22W Auto Gear | | | 18-080-020 |
| **A15  Mainshaft 3rd Gear** | | | |
| Gear L27-s36T: M20/M21 | 1963–1974 | 3831747 | 18-080-007 |
| Gear L27-s36T: M22 | 1965–1972 | 3880845 | 18-080-008 |
| Gear L26-s36T: M22W Auto Gear | | | 18-080-009 |
| Gear L25-s36T: M22Z Auto Gear | | | 18-080-012 |
| **A16  Mainshaft 3-4 Synchronizer Parts** | | | |
| Mainshaft synchronizer snap ring | All | 3831741 | 3831741 |
| Synchro ring w/o support shoulder - 2 req'd. | 1963–1965 | 3831733 | WT297-14 |
| Synchro ring w/support shoulder - 2 req'd. | 1966–1974 | 3880850 | WT297-14A |
| Synchro ring w/support shoulder, forged HD - 2 req'd. | 1966–1974 | 344243 | WT297-14D |
| Synchro hub | 1963–1965 | NSS | NSS |
| Synchro hub standard replacement | 1965–1974 | NSS | WT297-2.5A |
| Synchro hub hardened | | | 18-090-002 |
| Synchro hub hardened - oversize | | | 18-090-003 |
| Synchro hub hardened - oversize no key slots | | 18-090-004 | |
| Strut dog - 3 req'd. | All | 3915050 | WT297–1977 |
| Strut spring - 2 req'd., thin | 1963 | 591914 | N/A |
| Strut spring - 2 req'd., medium | 1964–1965 | 3853805 | N/A |
| Strut spring - 2 req'd., Wide | 1966–1974 | 3920775 | N/A |
| Strut spring- 2 req'd., modern replacement | 1963–1974 | 4682AJ | |
| Sliding clutch 36-spline | 1963–1974 | NSS | T85B-15 |
| Sliding clutch 36-spline, "torque-locking" | | | T85B-15A |
| Sliding clutch 18-spline, "slick shift lightened" | | | 18-089-001 |
| 3-4 synchronizer assembly | 1963–1974 | 357238 | 18-590-012 |
| 3-4 synchronizer assembly, "torque-locking" | 1963–1974 | | 18-590-014 |
| **A17  Mainshaft** | | | |
| *This shaft used with 1st-gear thrust washer:* | | | |
| Mainshaft 27-spline, 21.13" long | 1963 | 3831753 | WT297-2 |
| *These shafts used with 1st-gear bushing or roller bearing:* | | | |
| Mainshaft 27-spline, 27.50" long, Pontiac | 1964–1965 | 388838 | N/A |
| Mainshaft 27-spline, 21.13" long | 1964–1970 | 3915087 | 297-2A |
| Mainshaft 27-spline, 21.13" long, lightened | 1964–1970 | | 18-171-001 |
| Mainshaft 32-spline, 21.75" long | 1971–1975 | 3978759 | 297-2G |
| Mainshaft 32-spline, 21.75" long, lightened | 1971–1975 | | 18-171-002 |

| Group# | Description | Year | OEM# | Replacement # |
|---|---|---|---|---|
| A18 | **Mainshaft Extension Gasket** | | | |
| | Gasket | 1963–1974 | 3911901 | 18-045-104 |
| A19 | **Mainshaft Extension Housing Assembly** | | | |
| | *This is for GM Casting # 3831731 # 3846429:* | | | |
| | Housing: driver-side speedo, 27-spline | 1963–1970 | 3846428 | N/A |
| | *This is for GM Casting # 9779246:* | | | |
| | Housing: long 27-spline mainshaft, Pontiac | 1965–1968 | 9779245 | N/A |
| | *This is for GM Casting # 3857584:* | | | |
| | Housing: passenger-side speedo, 27-spline | 1966–1970 | 3857583 | N/A |
| | Housing: 27-spline, heavy-duty, Auto Gear | 1971–1974 | | 18-410-21 |
| | *This is for GM Casting # 3978764:* | | | |
| | Housing: passenger-side speedo, 32-spline | 1971–1974 | 3978763 | N/A |
| | Housing: 32-spline, heavy-duty, Auto Gear | 1971–1974 | | 18-410-22 |
| A20 | **Extension Housing Bushing** | | | |
| | 27-spline mainshaft | 1963–1970 | 6260048 | 6260048 |
| | 32-spline mainshaft | 1971–1974 | 3978765 | 3978765 |
| A21 | **Extension Housing Rear Seal** | | | |
| | 27-spline mainshaft | 1963–1970 | 1243402 | 15041CR |
| | 32-spline mainshaft | 1971–1974 | 8626009 | 18992CR |
| A22 | **Extension Housing Fasteners** | | | |
| | *These are used for stock housings:* | | | |
| | 3/8-16 x 1-3/4 HHCS SAE 5 - 3 req'd. | | | 88181995 |
| | 7/16-14 x 1-7/8 HHCS SAE 5 - 2 req'd. | | | 67435206 |
| | 7/16-14 x 2-1/2 HHCS SAE 5 - 1 req'd. | | | 67435321 |
| | *These are used for Auto Gear housings:* | | | |
| | 3/8-16 x 2 SHCS - 3 req'd. | | | 0-183-013 |
| | 3/8 split hi-collar washer - 3 req'd. | | | 0-047-009 |
| | 7/16-14 x 2 SHCS - 1 req'd. | | | 0-183-011 |
| | 7/16-14 x 2-1/2 SHCS - 2 req'd. | | | 0-183-014 |
| | 7/16 split hi-collar washer - 3 req'd. | | | 0-047-010 |
| | Breather port plug 1/4-18 NPT - 1 req'd. | | | 444-576 |
| A23 | **Extension Housing Breather** | | | |
| | Filtered breather vent: 1/4-18 NPT | | | FV102 |
| | Alloy breather vent: 1/4-18 NPT | | | 0-572-002 |

## Group B: Maindrive and Retainer

| Group# | Description | Year | OEM# | Replacement # |
|---|---|---|---|---|
| B1 | **Mainshaft Pilot Bearing Assembly** | | | |
| | 17 rollers with steel cage | 1963–1974 | 9419248 | JV44-1419 |
| B2A | **Maindrive Gear - Threaded Bearing Nut** | | | |
| | *These gears used with 10-spline clutch GM standard:* | | | |
| | Gear: L24-s36T: early M20 | 1963–1965 | 3831767 | WT297-16A |
| | Gear: L21-s36T: later M20 | 1966–1970 | 357241 | WT297-16B |
| | Gear: L26-s36T: M21 | 1963–1970 | 357242 | WT297-16 |
| | Gear: L26-s36T: M22 | 1963–1970 | 3925691 | WT297-16U |
| | *These gears are Auto Gear 10-spline clutch M22 gears; they have longer pilots to work with block plates and SuperCases:* | | | |
| | Gear: L22-s36T | M22Z | | 18-085-011 |
| | Gear: L24-s36T | M22W | | 18-085-009 |
| | Gear: L26-s36T | M22 | | 18-085-007 |

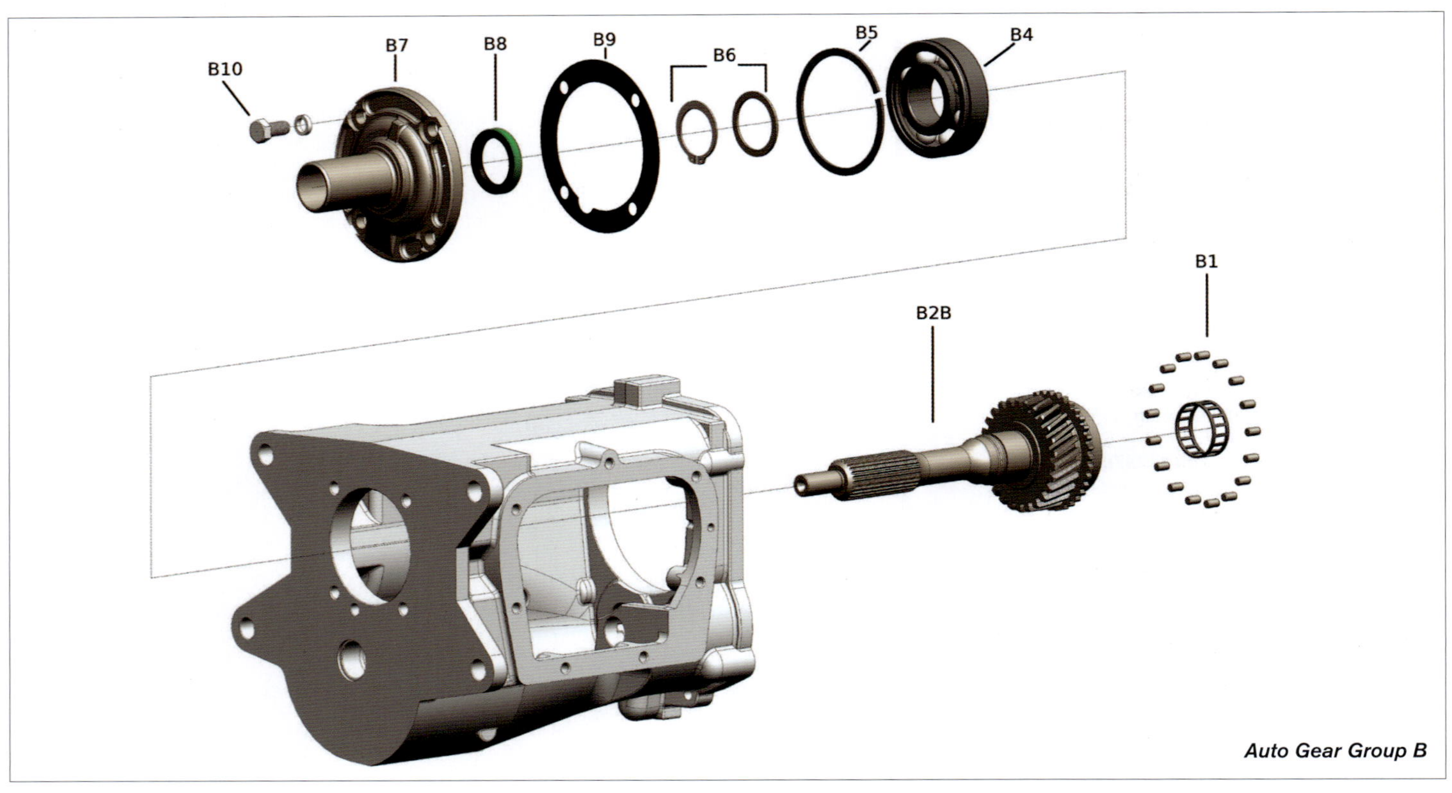



| Group# Description | Year | OEM# | Replacement # |
|---|---|---|---|
| *These gears used with 26-spline clutch GM standard:* | | | |
| Gear: L21-s36T: M20 | 1971–1974 | 3978772 | WT297-16C |
| Gear: L26-s36T: M21 | 1971–1974 | 357244 | WT297-16 |
| Gear: L26-s36T: M22 | 1971–1972 | 3978761 | WT297-16Z |
| | | | |
| *These gears are Auto Gear 26-spline clutch M22 gears; they have longer pilots to work with block plates and SuperCases:* | | | |
| Gear: L22-s36T: M22Z | | | 18-085-012 |
| Gear: L24-s36T: M22W | | | 18-085-010 |
| Gear: L26-s36T: M22 | | | 18-085-008 |
| **B2B** **Maindrive Gear - Front Seal Type** | | | |
| *These gears are Auto Gear 26-spline clutch M22 gears; they have longer pilots to work with block plates and SuperCases and use a front seal:* | | | |
| Gear: L22-s36T: M22Z: oil seal | | | 33-085-007 |
| Gear: L24-s36T: M22W: oil seal | | | 33-085-006 |
| Gear: L26-s36T: M22: oil seal | | | 33-085-005 |
| **B3** **Maindrive Oil Slinger** | | | |
| Slinger - used with threaded nut maindrives only | 1965–1974 | 3925692 | 18-036-001 |
| **B4** **Maindrive Front Bearing** | | | |
| NDH 47207 | 1963 | 907930 | 6207NR |
| NDH 41307B | 1964–1974 | 907572 | N307LOE |
| *These are used with Auto Gear SuperCase only:* | | | |
| SKF #6307NR | | | 6307NR |
| Nachi #6307-2NSENR | | | 0-130-019 |
| **B5** **Maindrive Bearing/Case Snap Ring** | | | |
| Bearing outer-locating snap ring | 1963 | 3707174 | 3707174 |
| Bearing outer-locating snap ring | 1964–1974 | 2830050 | 2830050 |
| **B6** **Bearing Retaining Nut/Snap Ring** | | | |
| Retaining nut | 1963–1974 | 591150 | 591150 |
| Snap ring w/oil seal maindrives | | | 0-139-29 |
| Snap-ring spacer w/oil seal maindrives: .062" thick | | 3709350 | 3709350 |

| Group# Description | Year | OEM# | Replacement # |
|---|---|---|---|
| **B7**   **Maindrive Front Bearing Retainer** | | | |
| w/6207NR bearing and nut | 1963 | 907930 | N/A |
| w/N307LOE bearing and nut | 1964–1974 | 3915020 | 3915020 |
| w/6307NR and oil seal | | | 18-027-002 |
| 5.125" truck adapter w/nut | | | 18-027-003 |
| 5.125" truck adapter w/seal | | | 18-027-004 |
| Machined for 3/8-16 SHCS - includes 4 cap screws | | | 18-027-007 |
| **B8**   **Maindrive Oil Seal** | | | |
| Front oil seal | | 3987936 | 12363CR |
| **B9**   **Maindrive Retainer Gasket** | | | |
| Gasket for 6207NR bearing | 1963 | 591023 | 591023 |
| Gasket: .030" thick | | 3915019 | 18-045-101 |
| Gasket: .015" thick | | | 18-045-105 |
| **B10**   **Maindrive Retainer Hardware** | | | |
| *These are used with standard retainers only; hardware for the 1963 retainer is not available:* | | | |
| 3/8-16 x 1" HHCS SAE 5 - 4 req'd. | 1964–1974 | 186678 | 05727102 |
| Bolt retainer lock plate, left | 1964–1974 | 3849937 | 3849937 |
| Bolt retainer lock plate, right | 1964–1974 | 3849938 | 3849938 |
| Lock-plate kit, both plates | 1964–1974 | | TSP-937 |
| *These are used with Auto Gear Supercases:* | | | |
| 3/8-16 x 1-1/8" HHCS SAE 8 - 4 req'd. | | | 67521047 |

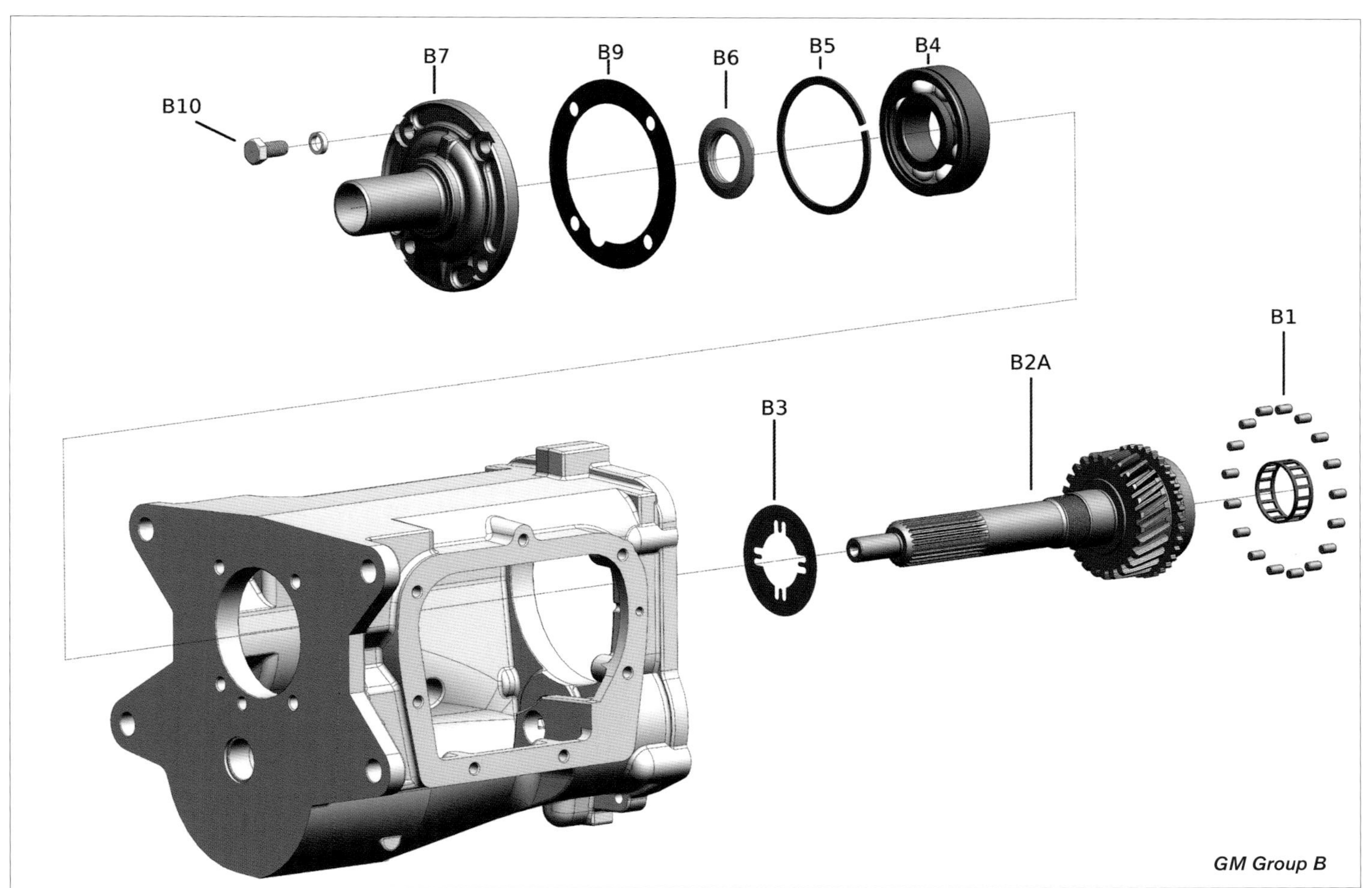

# Group C: Countershafts and Case

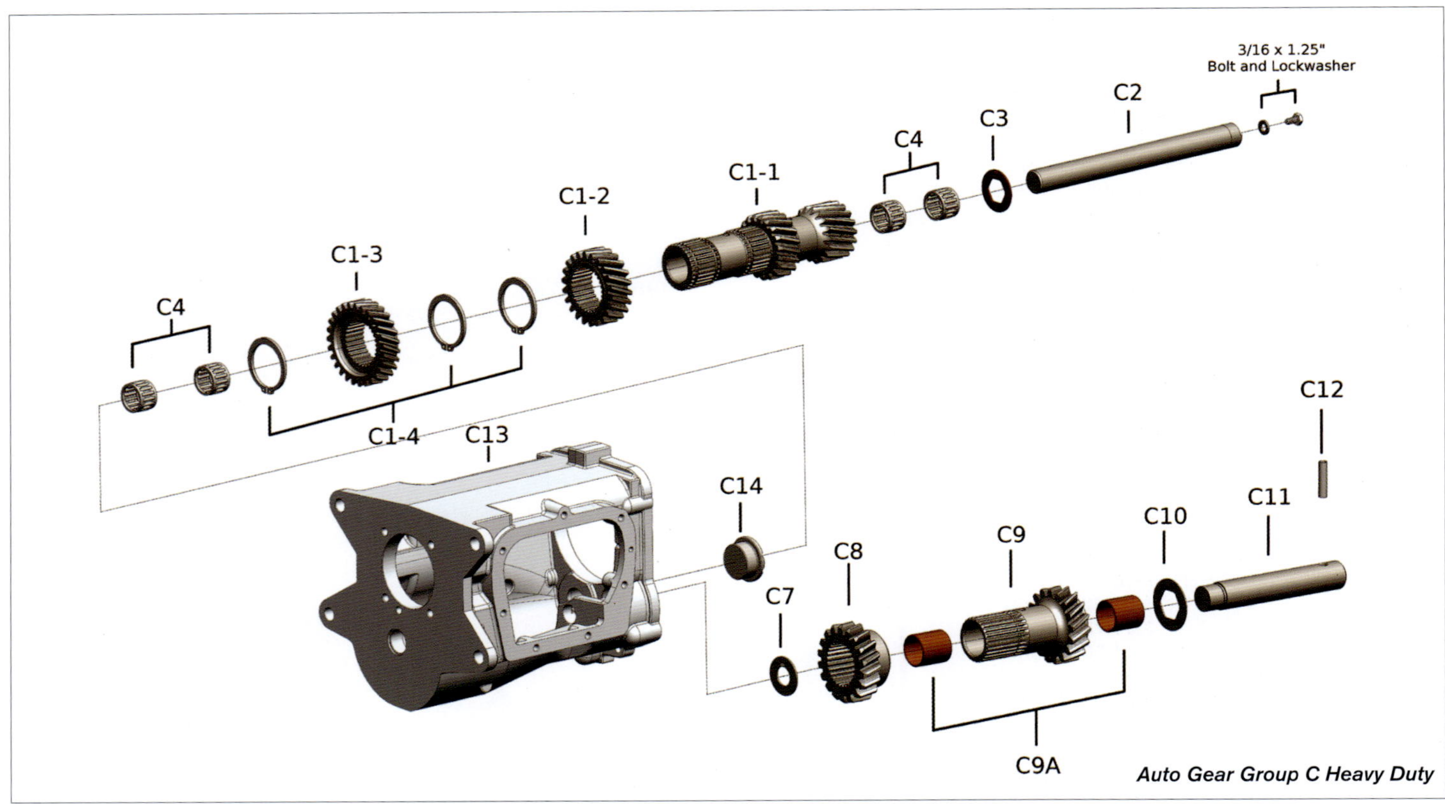


| Group# | Description | Year | OEM# | Replacement # |
|---|---|---|---|---|
| C1 | **Countershaft Cluster Gear** | | | |
| | *These gears are used with 7/8-inch countershaft:* | | | |
| | R27-22-19-17T M21 | 1963–1965 | 3831727 | WT297-8 |
| | R29-22-19-17T M20 | 1963–1965 | 3831728 | WT297-8A |
| | | | | |
| | *These gears are used with 1-inch countershaft:* | | | |
| | R25-22-19-17T M20 | 1966–1974 | 357235 | WT297-8C |
| | R27-22-19-17T M21 | 1966–1974 | 357236 | WT297-8D |
| | R27-22-19-17T M22 | 1966–1974 | 3905466 | WT297-8E |
| | | | | |
| | *These M22 gears are Auto Gear design with no spacer tube:* | | | |
| | R27-22-19-17T – 2.199/1.640/1.274/1.000 M22 | | | 18-077-001 |
| | R27-23-20-17T – 2.199/1.506/1.174/1.000 M22X | | | 18-077-002 |
| | R29-23-20-17T – 2.559/1.752/1.366/1.000 M22W | | | 18-077-003 |
| | R31-24-20-17T – 2.984/2.043/1.468/1.000 M22Z | | | 18-077-004 |
| | | | | |
| | *These M22 gears are Modular design with variable ratios:* | | | |
| | R27-22-19-17T – 2.199/1.640/1.274/1.000 | | | 18-567-111 |
| | R27-22-20-17T – 2.199/1.506/1.274/1.000 | | | 18-567-112 |
| | R27-23-19-17T – 2.199/1.640/1.174/1.000 | | | 18-567-121 |
| | R27-23-20-17T – 2.199/1.506/1.174/1.000 | | | 18-567-122 |
| | R27-24-19-17T – 2.199/1.640/1.082/1.000 | | | 18-567-131 |
| | R27-24-20-17T – 2.199/1.506/1.082/1.000 | | | 18-567-132 |
| | R29-22-19-17T – 2.559/1.908/1.483/1.000 | | | 18-567-211 |
| | R29-22-20-17T – 2.559/1.752/1.483/1.000 | | | 18-567-212 |
| | R29-23-19-17T – 2.559/1.908/1.366/1.000 | | | 18-567-221 |
| | R29-23-20-17T – 2.559/1.752/1.366/1.000 | | | 18-567-222 |
| | R29-24-19-17T – 2.559/1.908/1.259/1.000 | | | 18-567-231 |

| Group# Description | Year | OEM# | Replacement # |
|---|---|---|---|
| R29-24-20-17T – 2.559/1.752/1.259/1.000 | | | 18-567-232 |
| R31-22-19-17T – 2.984/2.225/1.729/1.000 | | | 18-567-311 |
| R31-22-20-17T – 2.984/2.043/1.729/1.000 | | | 18-567-312 |
| R31-23-19-17T – 2.984/2.225/1.593/1.000 | | | 18-567-321 |
| R31-23-20-17T – 2.984/2.043/1.593/1.000 | | | 18-567-322 |
| R31-24-19-17T – 2.984/2.225/1.468/1.000 | | | 18-567-331 |
| R31-24-20-17T – 2.984/2.043/1.468/1.000 | | | 18-567-332 |

*These M22 gears are Modular design, variable ratios, extreme-duty 8620 alloy:*

| Description | Year | OEM# | Replacement # |
|---|---|---|---|
| R27-22-19-16T – 2.207/1.640/1.274/1.000 | | | 18-567-113 |
| R27-23-19-16T – 2.207/1.640/1.174/1.000 | | | 18-567-123 |
| R27-24-19-16T – 2.207/1.640/1.082/1.000 | | | 18-567-133 |
| R29-22-19-16T – 2.568/1.908/1.483/1.000 | | | 18-567-213 |
| R29-23-19-16T – 2.568/1.908/1.366/1.000 | | | 18-567-223 |
| R29-24-19-16T – 2.568/1.908/1.259/1.000 | | | 18-567-233 |
| R31-22-19-16T – 2.994/2.225/1.729/1.000 | | | 18-567-313 |
| R31-23-19-16T – 2.994/2.225/1.593/1.000 | | | 18-567-323 |
| R31-24-19-16T – 2.994/2.225/1.468/1.000 | | | 18-567-333 |

*These M22 gears are Modular design, variable ratios, extreme-duty 9310 alloy 1-2 section:*

| Description | Year | OEM# | Replacement # |
|---|---|---|---|
| R27-22-19-16T – 2.207/1.640/1.274/1.000 | | | 18-567-114 |
| R27-22-20-16T – 2.207/1.506/1.274/1.000 | | | 18-567-115 |
| R27-23-19-16T – 2.207/1.640/1.174/1.000 | | | 18-567-124 |
| R27-23-20-16T – 2.207/1.506/1.174/1.000 | | | 18-567-125 |
| R27-24-19-16T – 2.207/1.640/1.082/1.000 | | | 18-567-134 |
| R27-24-20-16T – 2.207/1.506/1.082/1.000 | | | 18-567-135 |
| R29-22-19-16T – 2.568/1.908/1.483/1.000 | | | 18-567-214 |
| R29-22-20-16T – 2.568/1.752/1.483/1.000 | | | 18-567-215 |
| R29-23-19-16T – 2.568/1.908/1.366/1.000 | | | 18-567-224 |
| R29-23-20-16T – 2.568/1.752/1.366/1.000 | | | 18-567-225 |
| R29-24-19-16T – 2.568/1.908/1.259/1.000 | | | 18-567-234 |
| R29-24-20-16T – 2.568/1.752/1.259/1.000 | | | 18-567-235 |
| R31-22-19-16T – 2.994/2.225/1.729/1.000 | | | 18-567-314 |
| R31-22-20-16T – 2.994/2.043/1.729/1.000 | | | 18-567-315 |
| R31-23-19-16T – 2.994/2.225/1.593/1.000 | | | 18-567-324 |
| R31-23-20-16T – 2.994/2.043/1.593/1.000 | | | 18-567-325 |
| R31-24-19-16T – 2.994/2.225/1.468/1.000 | | | 18-567-334 |
| R31-24-20-16T – 2.994/2.043/1.468/1.000 | | | 18-567-335 |

**C1-1 Countershaft 1st/2nd-Gear M22, Heavy-Duty**

| Description | Year | OEM# | Replacement # |
|---|---|---|---|
| S30-R19-17T | | | 18-067-001 |
| S30-R20-17T | | | 18-067-002 |

**C1-1 Countershaft 1st/2nd-Gear M23, Extreme-Duty**

| Description | Year | OEM# | Replacement # |
|---|---|---|---|
| S30-R19-16T SAE 8620 equivalent | | | 18-067-003 |
| S30-R19-16T SAE 9310 equivalent | | | 18-067-004 |
| S30-R20-16T SAE 9310 equivalent | | | 18-067-005 |

**C1-2 Countershaft 3rd Gear**

| Description | Year | OEM# | Replacement # |
|---|---|---|---|
| R22-S30T | | | 18-070-010 |
| R23-S30T | | | 18-070-020 |
| R24-S30T | | | 18-070-030 |

**C1-3 Countershaft Drive Gear**

| Description | Year | OEM# | Replacement # |
|---|---|---|---|
| R27-S30t | | | 18-070-100 |
| R29-S30t | | | 18-070-200 |
| R31-S30t | | | 18-070-300 |

**C1-4 Countershaft Gear/Shaft Snap Rings**

| Description | Year | OEM# | Replacement # |
|---|---|---|---|
| Retaining Ring - 3 req'd. | | | 0-139-031 |

**C2 Countershaft**

| Description | Year | OEM# | Replacement # |
|---|---|---|---|
| 7/8" diameter | 1963–1965 | 3831725 | Wt297-3 |
| 1" diameter | 1966–1974 | 3864850 | WT297-3A |
| 1" diameter - locks to Auto Gear midplate | | | 18-068-014 |

| Group# Description | Year | OEM# | Replacement # |
|---|---|---|---|
| **C3**   **Countershaft Thrust Washer** | | | |
| 7/8" diameter - 2 req'd. | 1963–1965 | 3831729 | 3831729 |
| 1" diameter - 2 req'd., Babbitt | 1966–1974 | 3864860 | 3864860 |
| 1" diameter - 2 req'd., steel-backed bronze | 1966–1974 | | 18-193-001 |
| **C4**   **Countershaft Bearings** | | | |
| 7/8"-diameter shaft - 80 req'd. | 1963–1965 | 3709328 | S443Q |
| 1"-diameter shaft - 112 req'd. | 1966–1974 | 435847 | C407Q |
| Unit cages - 4 req'd. | | | 18-132-001 |
| **C5**   **Countershaft Roller Spacer** | | | |
| 7/8" diameter - 6 req'd. | 1963–1965 | 3709324 | 3709324 |
| 1" diameter - 6 req'd. | 1966–1974 | 3864856 | 3864856 |
| **C6**   **Countershaft Spacer Tube** | | | |
| 7/8" diameter | 1963–1965 | N/A | N/A |
| 1" diameter | 1966–1974 | 3912195 | 3912195 |
| **C7**   **Idler Gear Front Thrust Washer** | | | |
| Steel-backed bronze | 1963–1974 | 3834739 | 18-193-003 |
| **C8**   **Idler Gear Front** | | | |
| L18-s27T: M20/M21 | 1963–1974 | 3831762 | WT297-10 |
| L18-s27T: M22 | 1965–1972 | 3879997 | 18-084-003 |
| L17-s27T: M23 | | | 18-084-004 |
| **C9**   **Idler Gear Rear** | | | |
| L17-27T with bushings | 1963–1974 | 3831764 | 18-584-001 |
| **C9a**   **Idler Gear Bushings** | | | |
| Bronze bushing - 2 req'd. | 1963–1974 | NSS | T10-85AS |
| **C10**   **Idler Gear Rear Thrust Washer** | | | |
| Steel washer | 1963–1974 | 3774909 | 3774909 |

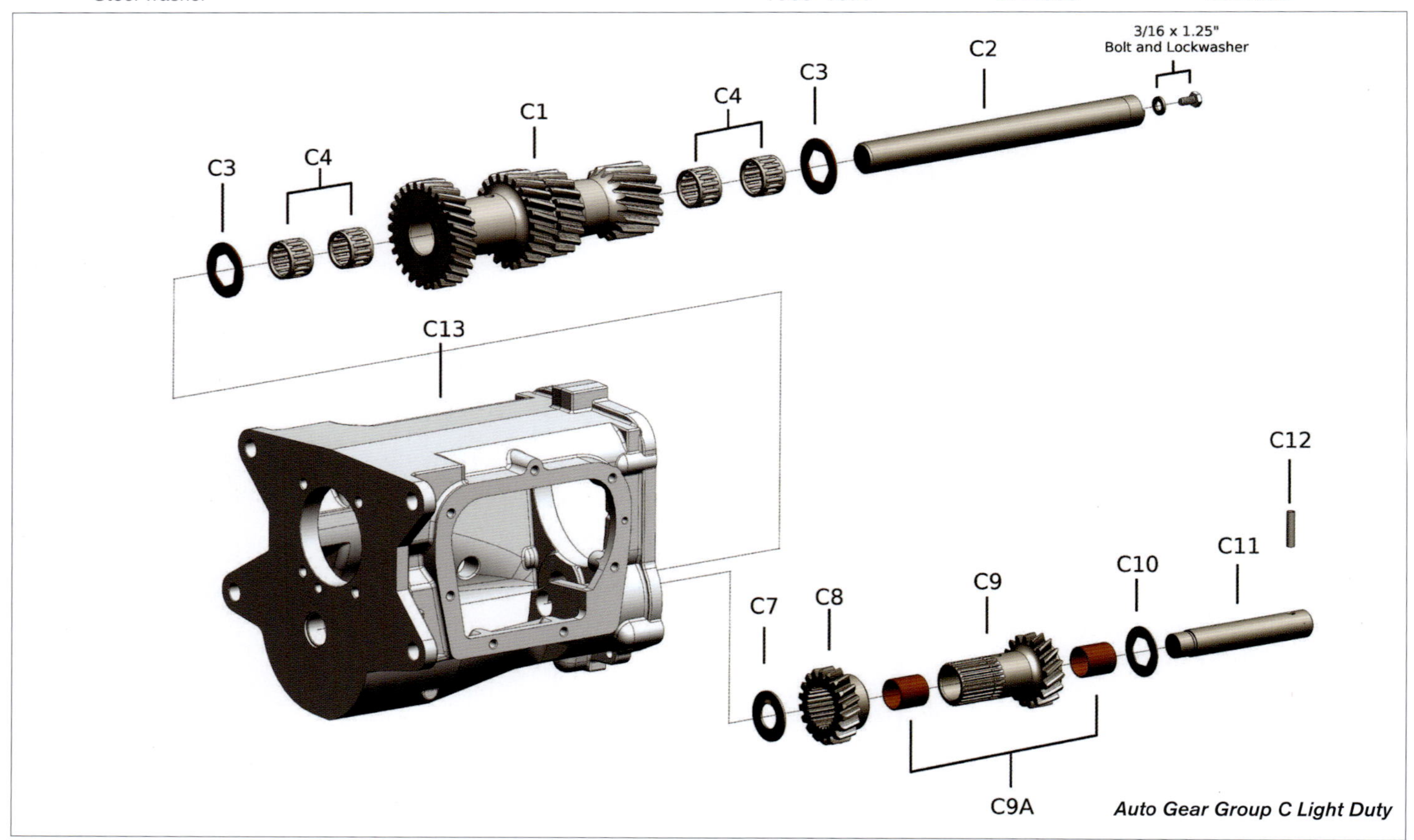

| Group# Description | Year | OEM# | Replacement # |
|---|---|---|---|
| **C11** **Reverse Idler Shaft** | | | |
| Shaft w/o lock pin | 1963–1974 | 3831761 | WT297-35 |
| **C12** **Idler Shaft Lock Pin** | | | |
| Split pin: 1/4" diameter x 1.5" long | 1963–1974 | 590832 | 590832 |
| **C13** **Main Case Assembly** | | | |
| *These cases are used with a 7/8" countershaft:* | | | |
| Casting #3831704 w/6207N Bearing | 1963 | 3831702 | N/A |
| Casting #3851325 | 1964–1965 | 3851324 | N/A |
| Auto Gear SuperCase for 7/8" shaft | | | 18-065-001 |
| *These cases are used with a 1" countershaft:* | | | |
| Casting #3885010 | 1966–1967 | | 3925659 |
| #3925660 | 1968–1970 | | 3925659 |
| #3925661 | 1970–1974 | | 3925659 |
| Auto Gear SuperCase for 1" shaft | | | 18-065-002 |
| Auto Gear SuperCase for 1" shaft w/thrust button | | | 18-565-001 |
| **C14** **Case Hardware** | | | |
| Thrust button | | | 18-193-004 |
| Countershaft plug: 1-1/8" diameter | | | 0-113-011 |
| Fill-plug SuperCase-only hex head | | | 0-052-014 |
| Fill-plug SuperCase-only socket head | | | 0-052-012 |
| Drain-plug SuperCase-only hex head, magnetic | | | 0-052-015 |
| Drain-plug SuperCase-only socket head, magnetic | | | 0-052-013 |

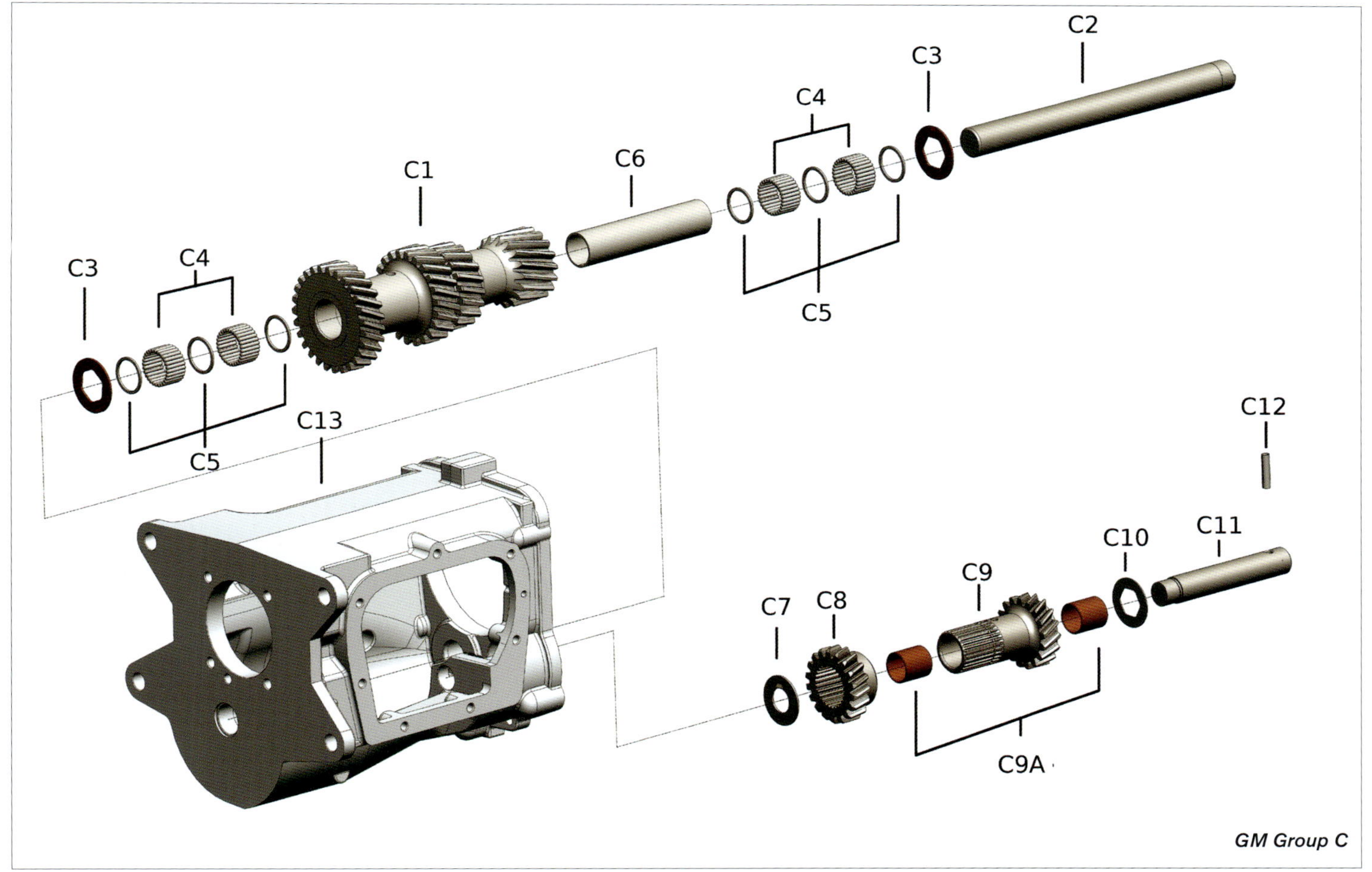

# Group D: Internal Shift Linkage

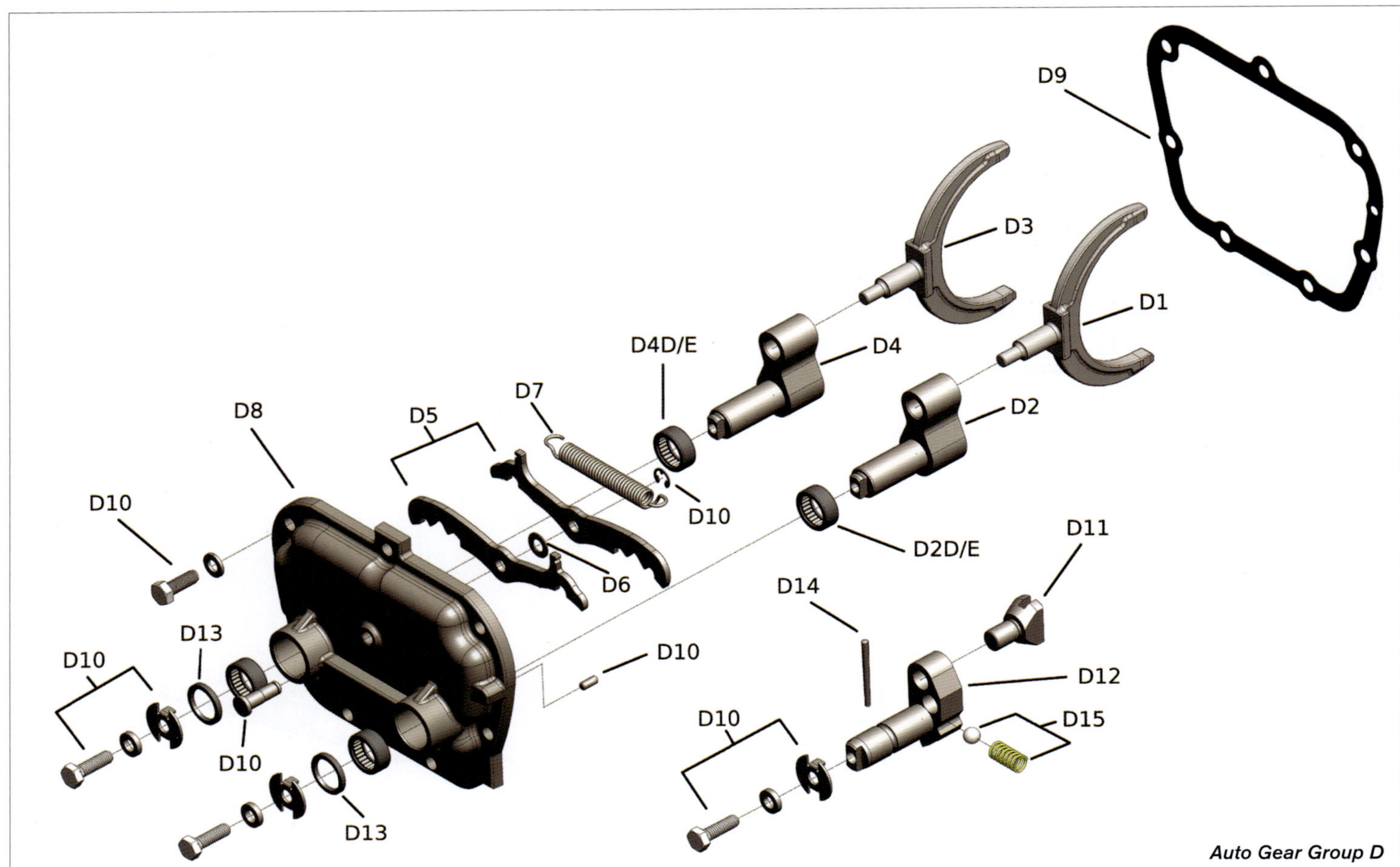



| Group# | Description | Year | OEM# | Replacement # |
|---|---|---|---|---|
| **D1** | **1st and 2nd Shift Fork** | | | |
| | Nodular iron - OEM style | 1963–1974 | 3831717 | 3831717 |
| | Investment cast steel - Auto Gear design | All | | 18-096-005 |
| | | | | |
| **D2** | **1st and 2nd Lever Assembly** | | | |
| | 5/16-18 external-thread stud | 1963–1968 | 3831709 | N/A |
| | 3/8-16 internal-thread w/o switch | 1969 | 3950308 | N/A |
| | 3/8-16 internal-thread w/switch | 1969–1974 | 3952649 | N/A |
| | 5/16-24 internal-thread welded universal HD | All | | 18-598-001-2x |
| D2A | Linkage-arm adapter for older 3/8" bolt-on arms | | | 18-040-001 |
| D2B | 5/16-24 X 1 HHCS Grade-8 for use w/welded lever | | | 67531483 |
| D2C | 5/16 Grade-8 split lock washer | | | 05724810 |
| D2D | Bushing | | | 6454045 |
| D2E | Roller bearing | | | B-126 |
| | | | | |
| **D3** | **3rd and 4th Shift Fork** | | | |
| | Nodular iron - OEM style | 1963–1974 | 3831717 | 3831717 |
| | Investment cast steel - Auto Gear design | All | | 18-096-005 |
| | | | | |
| **D4** | **3rd and 4th Lever Assembly** | | | |
| | 5/16-18 external-thread stud | 1963–1968 | 3831709 | N/A |
| | 3/8-16 internal-thread w/switch | 1968 | 3950472 | N/A |
| | 3/8-16 internal-thread w/o switch | 1969 | 3950308 | N/A |
| | 3/8-16 internal-thread w/switch | 1969–1974 | 3952649 | N/A |
| | 5/16-24 24 internal-thread welded universal HD | All | | 18-598-001-2x |

| Group# | Description | Year | OEM# | Replacement # |
|---|---|---|---|---|
| D4A | Linkage-arm adapter for older 3/8" bolt-on arms | | | 18-040-001 |
| D4B | 5/16-24 X 1 HHCS Grade-8 for use w/welded lever | | | 67531483 |
| D4C | 5/16 Grade-8 split lock washer | | | 05724810 |
| D4D | Bushing | | | 6454045 |
| D4E | Roller bearing | | | B-126 |
| **D5** | **Detent Cam Levers** | | | |
| | Detent cam - 2 req'd. | All | 3905462 | 18-014-001 |
| **D6** | **Detent Cam Washer** | | | |
| | Hardened flat washer - Auto Gear cover only | | | 18-047-001 |
| **D7** | **Detent Cam Spring** | | | |
| | 20-pound detent spring | 1963–1974 | 3831718 | 18-156-002 |
| **D8** | **Shift Cover Assembly** | | | |
| | *These covers used with externally threaded shift lever assemblies:* | | | |
| | Casting #3831707 | 1963–1965 | 3831707 | N/A |
| | Casting #3884685 | 1966–1970 | 3895778 | N/A |
| | *These covers used with internally threaded shift lever assemblies:* | | | |
| | Casting #3950306: short boss w/o TCS switch | 1970–1974 | 3977618 | N/A |
| | Casting #3952648: short boss w/TCS switch | 1970–1974 | 3952647 | N/A |
| | Casting #3952642: long boss w/TCS switch | 1970–1974 | 335308 | N/A |
| | *Use Auto Gear universal cover assembly to replace above:* | | | |
| | Auto Gear cover assembly includes cams, shafts, seals, pivot, spring | | | 18-410-023-2x |

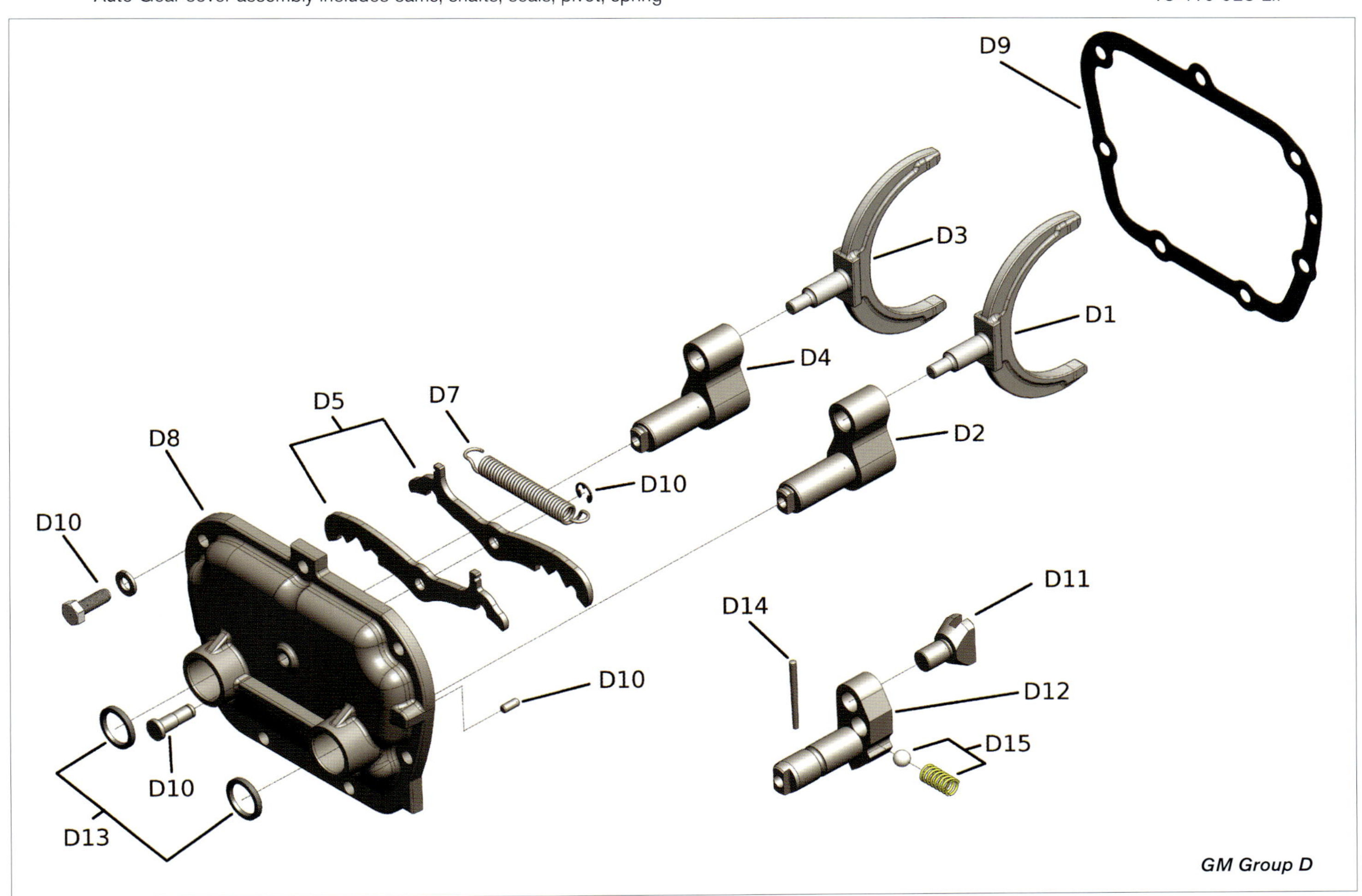

| Group# | Description | Year | OEM# | Replacement # |
|---|---|---|---|---|
| **D9** | **Shift Cover Gasket** | | | |
| | Cover gasket | 1963–1974 | 3831705 | 3831705 |
| **D10** | **Shift Cover Hardware** | | | |
| | Cover bolts: 5/16-18 x 3/4 HHCS - 7 req'd. | All | 05726070 | |
| | Split lockwashers: 5/16" diameter - 7 req'd. | All | NSS | 05724810 |
| | Cover shift shaft seal - 2 req'd. | 1963–1974 | 3831716 | 7410CR |
| | Pivot pin | 1963–1974 | 3884686 | 18-043-002 |
| | C-clip | NSS | 0-139-020 | |
| | Dowel pin: 3/16" diameter x 3/8" long | | NSS | 40630212 |
| | TCS switch plug | | 3906448 | N/A |
| | TCS switch plug gasket | | 3906462 | N/A |
| **D11** | **Reverse Shift Fork** | | | |
| | Reverse fork | 1963–1974 | 3832786 | 18-096-003 |
| **D12** | **Reverse Shift Lever Assembly** | | | |
| | 5/16-18 external thread | 1963–1968 | 3850086 | N/A |
| | 3/8-16 internal thread | 1969–1974 | 3950312 | N/A |
| | Auto Gear universal lever assembly | All | | 18-598-002-2x |
| **D13** | **Lever Oil Seal** | | | |
| | Oil seal: 2 for cover, 1 for extension | 1963–1974 | 3831716 | 7410CR |
| **D14** | **Reverse Shifter Lock Pin** | | | |
| | Tapered lock pin: #0 size, 1-1/4" long | 1963–1974 | 103565 | 0-125 |
| **D15** | **Reverse Detent Ball and Spring** | | | |
| | Detent spring | 1963–1974 | 3773017 | 3773017 |
| | Detent ball: 3/8" diameter | 1963–1974 | NSS | 00072744 |

# Group E: Service Kits

| Group# | Description | Year | OEM# | Replacement # |
|---|---|---|---|---|
| **E1** | **Small Parts Kit** | | | |
| | *Small parts include needle bearings, snap rings, thrust washers, pins, and spacers:* | | | |
| | 7/8" diameter countershaft | 1963–1965 | NSS | SP297-50 |
| | 1" diameter countershaft | 1966–1974 | NSS | SP297-50A |
| **E2** | **Gasket and Seal Kit** | | | |
| | Gasket and seal kit: fits all years | | NSS | 297-GS1 |
| **E3** | **Overhaul Kit** | | | |
| | *Kits include main bearings, countershaft, synchro rings, all small parts, struts and springs, gaskets, bushing, and seals:* | | | |
| | Kit w/7/8" countershaft w/6207NR bearing | 1963 | | BK-297–1963 |
| | Kit w/7/8" countershaft w/N307LOE bearing | 1964–1965 | | BK-297 |
| | Kit w/1" countershaft | 1966–1974 | | BK-297A |

# *ORIGINAL MUNCIE PATENT ILLUSTRATIONS*

May 7, 1963  J. W. FODREA  3,088,336

TRANSMISSION

Original Filed Nov. 29, 1957  3 Sheets—Sheet 1

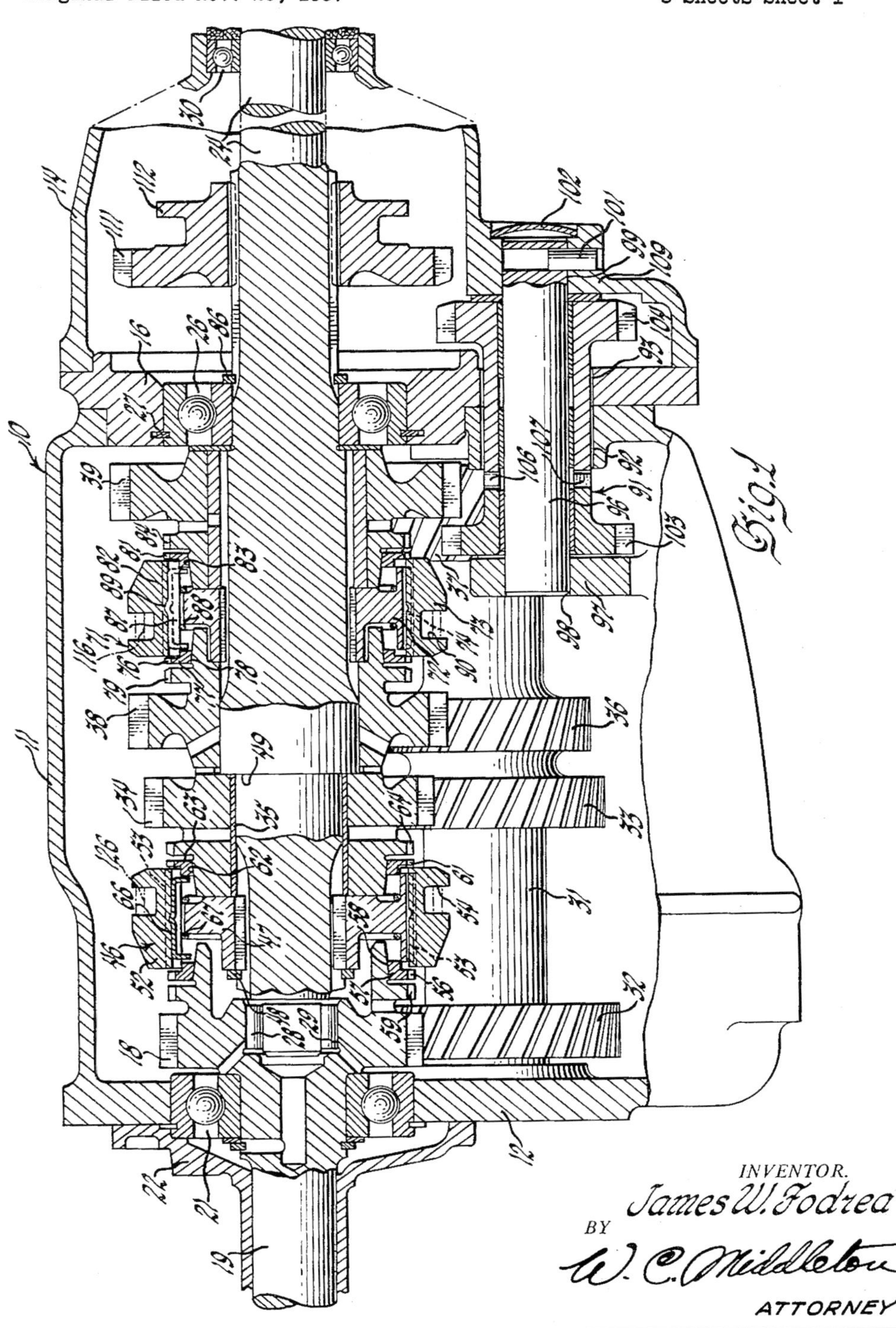


INVENTOR.
James W. Fodrea
BY
W. C. Middleton
ATTORNEY

**May 7, 1963** J. W. FODREA **3,088,336**

TRANSMISSION

Original Filed Nov. 29, 1957 3 Sheets-Sheet 2

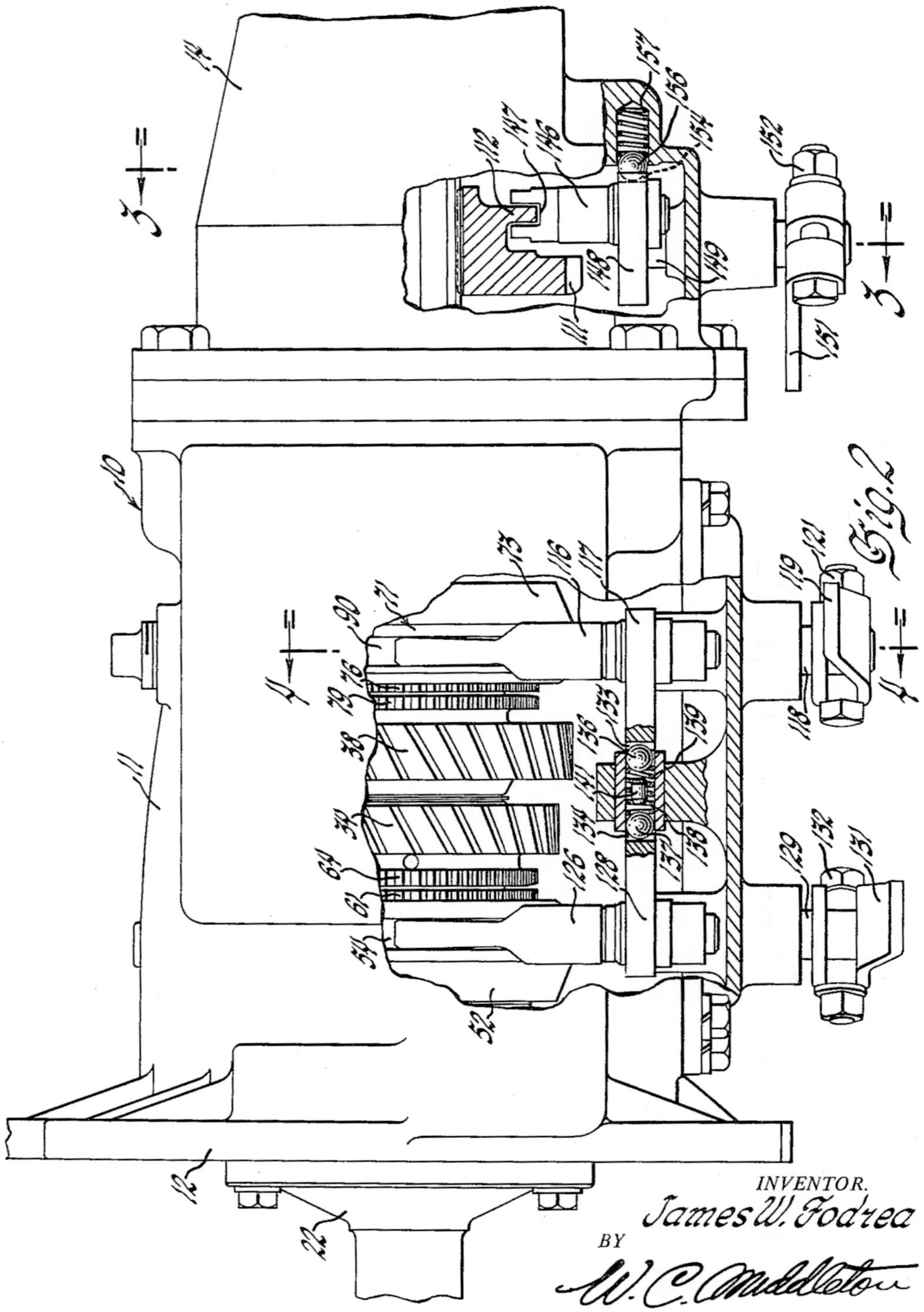


INVENTOR.
James W. Fodrea
BY
W. C. Middleton
ATTORNEY

May 7, 1963     J. W. FODREA     3,088,336

TRANSMISSION

Original Filed Nov. 29, 1957     3 Sheets—Sheet 3

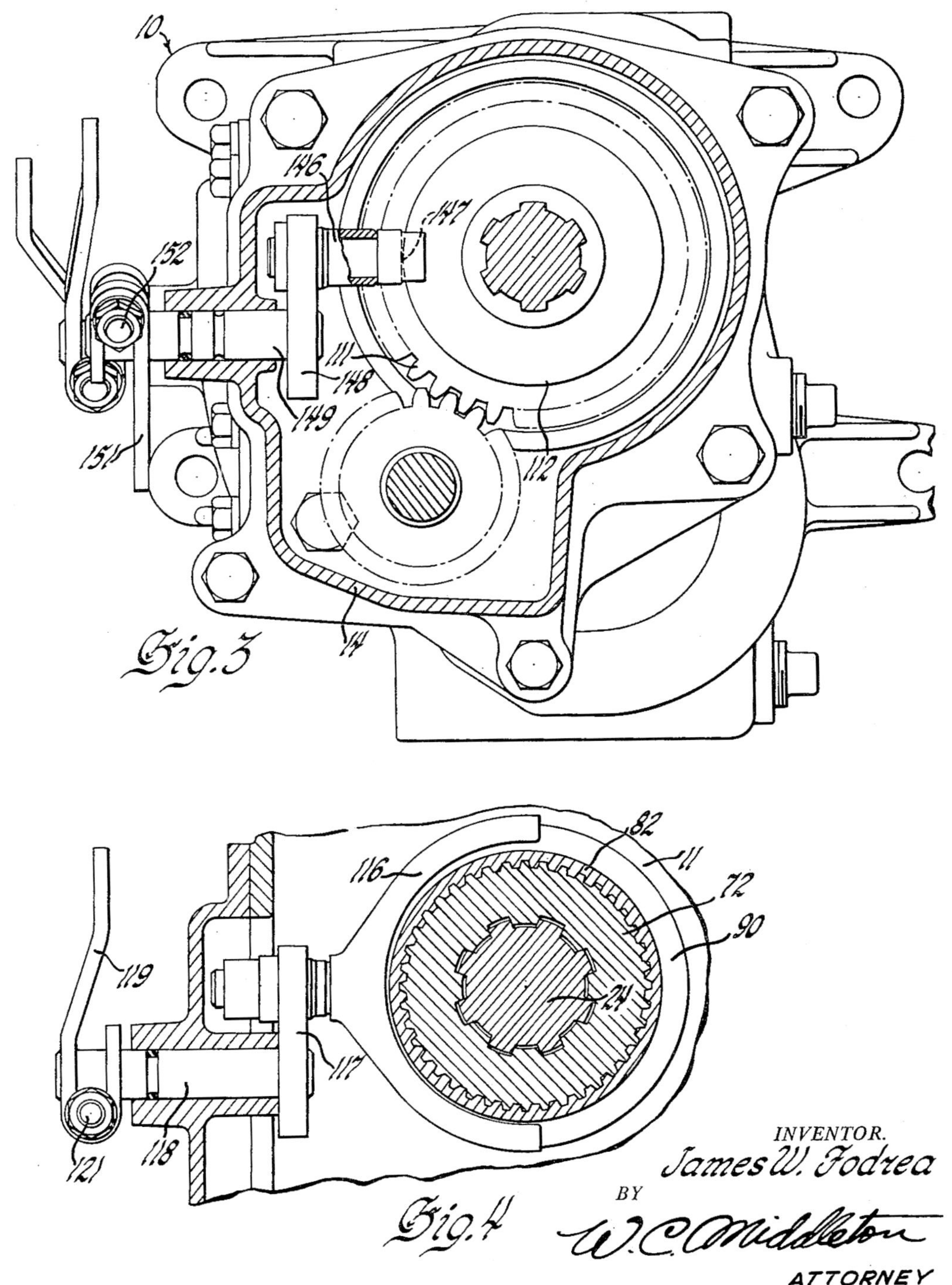

5SPEEDS.COM
208 N. U.S. Hwy. 1, Unit 1
Tequesta, FL 33469
561-743-5600
5speeds.com

Centerforce Clutches
2266 Crosswind Dr.
Prescott, AZ 86301
928-771-8411
centerforce.com

Crash Enterprises
9115 Old Green Bay Rd.
Pleasant Prairie, WI 53158
262-942-8882
crash_enterprises@yahoo.com

D&L Transmission
180 W. 19th St.
Huntington Station, NY 11746
631-351-4837
dandltransmission.com

Ed Hartnett Transmissions
242 Pembroke Ave.
Lansdowne, PA 19050
610-623-9381
eh4speeds@aol.com

Hurst Shifters
100 Stony Point Rd., Ste. 125
Santa Rosa, CA 95401
707-544-4761
hurst-shifters.com

Jody's Transmissions
141 W. 39th St.
Reading, PA 19606
jodystransmissions@verizon.net

Liberty's Gears
6309 Pelham Rd.
Taylor, MI 48180
313-278-4040
libertysgears.com

Long Shifters
150 N. Grant St.
Cleona, PA 17042
717-202-8374
g-forcetransmissions.com

Roltek Transmissions
371 Prospect Ave.
Hartland, WI 53029
262-369-0440
roltektrans.com

SK Tranny Shop
1075 Rt. 109
Lindenhurst, NY 11757
631-957-9427
skspeed.com

Steve Bechtold
306 Ocean Ave.
Northport, NY 11768
631-754-2285

The Wright Connection
3512 Caraway Ct
Bakersfield, CA 93309
661-304-1967
craig@wrightconnection.net

**BONUS CONTENT**

**Rebuild and Reassembly Video Links**

View a complete rebuild and reassembly four-part video series on Paul Cangialosi's GearBoxVideo YouTube channel.

Part 1

Part 2

Part 3

Part 4